ULTIMATE BETRAYAL

RECOGNIZING, UNCOVERING, AND DEALING WITH INFIDELITY

ULTIMATE BETRAYAL

RECOGNIZING, UNCOVERING, AND DEALING WITH INFIDELITY

DANINE MANETTE

SQUAREONE
PUBLISHERS

Cover Designer: Jacqueline Michelus
Typesetter: Gary A. Rosenberg
In-House Editors: Joanne Abrams and Marie Caratozzolo

Square One Publishers
115 Herricks Road
Garden City Park, NY 11040
(516) 535-2010 • (866) 900-BOOK
www.squareonepublishers.com

Library of Congress Cataloging-in-Publication Data

Manette, Danine.
   Ultimate betrayal : recognizing, uncovering, and dealing with infidelity /
Danine Manette.
     p. cm.
   Includes index.
   ISBN 0-7570-0281-1
1. Adultery—Psychological aspects. 2. Man-woman relationships. I. Title.

   HQ806.M353   2005
   306.73'6—dc22

                                                        2005009721

Printed in the United States of America

10   9   8   7   6   5   4   3   2   1

Contents

To my sister Dawna,
who dances with the angels.

Acknowledgments

Thank you, Lord Jesus, for giving me courage, strength, and peace—without which, where would I be? You promised me that no weapon formed against me shall prosper, and I have claimed the victory in Your name.

To my girls, Crystal, Deon, Sarah, Roz, Margo, Niki, Linda, and my sister Denise: Thanks for proofreading, listening, loving, hugging, caring, and watching my back. I love you and I am so blessed to have you in my life.

To my family: Mom and Dad, thanks for raising me to be a strong, independent, self-reliant, motivated woman who never has to "settle" for *anything*; Ryant, thanks for supporting me in this project and for encouraging me to see it through into fruition; Ryan, thanks for giving me a reason to wake up in the morning and for being a daily reminder of why I must forever remain healthy and sane; and Cedric, thanks for bringing everlasting love, joy, and happiness into my world each day with your kind and gentle spirit.

To my editors, Carolyn and Beatrice: Thanks! I most certainly could not have done this without you. I cannot begin to tell you how much I appreciate your time and input.

To my friend Melvin, the inspiration behind this book: Thanks for the motivation and for having unfaltering confidence and belief in me, even after all of these years.

To the fellas, Jahmal, George, Ernest, and Yusef: Thanks for the male perspective. I'll bet you didn't know I was taking notes during all of those conversations, did you?

To my fan club, Nicole and Stacey: Thanks for buying my book when it was only available on the Internet. You two changed my status from a writer to an author.

To Dr. David Miller: Thanks for helping me realize the difference between what I can control and what I cannot. I owe you my sanity.

To all my allies: You know who you are! Thanks for caring enough about me and my mental stability to place yourselves out on a limb in order to redirect my reality and preserve my dignity. I will always be indebted to you! I love you all!

Who Should Read This Book?

This book is for all those who have ever had a broken heart.

For those who have given themselves completely to another human being, offering pure and unconditional love from the core of their souls, only to have it thrown back at them.

For those who have cried themselves to sleep at night only to discover more tears awaiting them in the morning.

For those who believed, trusted, and gave of themselves freely, only to be used and deceived.

For those who have gone day after day with knots in their stomachs.

For those who have burst into tears, wondering if they were second choice.

For those who have battled mental ghosts each and every day as they crept up to overtake their thoughts.

And finally, for those who think that they will never love, never trust, or never feel again.

ULTIMATE
BETRAYAL

Introduction

J ust as many human beings know the joys of love, many share
the anguish that results from infidelity. In fact, it is astonishing
that something which has caused such widespread pain and
suffering to so many is practiced on such a regular basis, often by
its own victims. Nothing is more heart-wrenching or sickening than
the knowledge that your soul mate and true love has betrayed you.
And nothing is more torturous than the mental images that follow
such betrayal. Scars left by the wound of deception can have a far-
reaching effect in the areas of work, family, and—most especially—
future relationships.

But in my years of personal experience and working as an investigator, I have found that the healthiest way to deal with betrayal is to learn the truth and face the reality, no matter how painful it
may be. Only then can you take control of your life and move
towards a happier future.

HOW WE COPE WITH BETRAYAL

Everyone is unique in her own way. We are all individuals, with very individual ways of dealing with the challenges that life has to offer. Nevertheless, in my experience, I have found that there are three basic reactions to infidelity.

The individuals at one end of the spectrum use the experience of being betrayed as a way to uplift themselves and press forward. These are the people who can move on and never look back, not questioning for a moment the decision to sever ties, but always trusting their own instincts and intuition. They know that they are worthy of the quality of love they give to others, and they refuse to settle for anything less. They know how and when to walk away from a relationship, and can recognize when the games of others threaten their own mental stability and inner peace.

On the opposite end of the spectrum are those individuals who are crippled by the knowledge that the one they love has betrayed them. These are the people who would rather walk through life blindly than acknowledge what is sometimes literally right before their eyes. They are so horrified by the prospect of being alone that they are willing to settle for just about anything in order to have somebody in their lives, and they hang on, often years after the relationship has truly ended. They never walk away; they must be pushed. They accept what they are given rather than fighting for what they want, and they shield themselves from the reality of their situation.

Finally, there are the people in the middle of the spectrum—probably, the vast majority of the population. These are the people who place a great deal of trust in their mates, but not to the point of being blind. Although they don't look for trouble, they do not ignore it when it comes calling. They fear being the "last one to know" of betrayal, firmly believe that they would leave any mate who was unfaithful to them, and often criticize those who try to repair a relationship ravaged by infidelity. In truth, they are not as strong and self-reliant as the first group discussed. Yet they want to know what's going on—even if it hurts.

This book, of course, was designed for people who want to know if their mate is betraying them. In other words it was designed for the first and third groups discussed above—for people who want to know the truth even if they are afraid of the pain it might cause. But if you belong to the second group of individuals—if you are someone who doesn't feel strong enough to cope with the anguish of infidelity—I urge you to seek the strength that is within you, or to look for strength and support in friends, family, a group, or God. Although you may believe that the truth will destroy you, instead, it can help you break out of the cycle of betrayal and self-delusion, and seek a healthier way of life.

THE PURPOSE OF THIS BOOK

So many people are attuned to the telltale signs of betrayal. They are quick to sense when something "funny" is going on. But they cannot walk away from a relationship simply on a hunch. When their husband claims that the underwear in his car is his sister's; when their new guy insists that his brother asked him to rent that hotel room; when their boyfriend states that he doesn't know why some girl is sending him romantic cards, these people hesitate, still believing that their relationship is genuine and true. Before they take a step, they want proof.

Many of these people would love to hire a private detective or gain access to modern computerized surveillance technology. But for most, this is simply not an option. What they need are techniques that can easily and effectively be used to uncover the truth. That's what this book is all about. Not only are the methods presented within these pages easy to understand and follow, but they have been field-tested by women just like you—women who want proof before they take that next crucial step. Moreover, at the end of this book, you'll find a list of support groups that can help you every step of the way.

I applaud your desire to learn the truth, and I wish you the best of luck.

CHAPTER 1

Recognizing the Signs

S ince you're reading this book, there's a good chance that you've begun to wonder if something is going on with your mate. You're not sure, but you have that "funny feeling." He has begun to be absent for extended blocks of time; the phone keeps ringing, but when you answer, it's often a "wrong number"; or perhaps some of his stories just don't sound right to you. After finding they've been betrayed, many women report that there were in fact many signs of infidelity, but that they didn't bother to pay attention to them. They say that if they had taken the time to follow up on some of the clues they'd stumbled across, they would have known what was happening far sooner.

If you have decided that you want to know what's really going on in your relationship—either to satisfy your own desire for the truth, or as a means of building a case and eventually confronting your partner—this chapter will start you on your journey. In the following pages, you will begin to follow a step-by-step plan in which you collect and "file" potential evidence. The first phase of this plan is to perform a complete evaluation of your mate, yourself, and your relationship.

EVALUATING YOUR MATE'S HISTORY

In order to determine the likelihood that your mate is cheating on you, it is important to understand his history. You may need to utilize several methods to obtain this information, but very often, it's possible to get the information you need directly from your partner. During the course of your relationship, you have undoubtedly learned a great deal about both his character and the caliber of his past relationships. What if he has not been particularly forthcoming with such information? In that case, you probably know someone who was familiar with your mate before you met him—someone who would not be suspicious if you initiated a "matter-of-fact" conversation regarding your mate's prior relationships. Try to pose your questions as innocently as possible: "Kelly was a fool to let him go; why did they break up, anyway?" This sort of inquiry will probably not arouse the other person's suspicions, especially if you control your body language and tone of voice to avoid seeming overly interested.

The ultimate purpose of your questions is to assess exactly why your mate's prior relationships ended. You need to discover whether he has a history of being unfaithful to previous girlfriends or wives. Perhaps he denies being unfaithful, and reports instead that his earlier mates did not properly understand him or had too many "hang-ups." Perhaps he claims that they kept trying to "control" him. If you have heard any of these weak, tired lines, stay alert! Chances are that if a person has a history of infidelity, he has serious character issues and is a poor relationship risk. Be aware, too, that there's a difference between his having cheated on one person in the past, and his having had a series of relationships that ended as a result of infidelity.

As you explore your mate's previous relationships, be sure to discover how he dealt with the seeming inadequacies of each partner. For example, when she "didn't properly understand him," what did he do? When she had "hang-ups," what were they and how did he react? In what areas was she trying to control him? Was she trying to keep him from hanging out at bars or chit-chatting with his ex on the phone? And how did he respond to her attempts at control? If he in any way indicates that his past mate drove him to infidelity, that is a bad sign. The fact of the matter is that if a relationship is truly that unpleasant, a person of high character chooses dissolution rather than deception.

Perhaps your mate was cheating *with* you during his last relationship and you are wondering if he is currently doing the same thing *to* you now. If that is the case, you are very likely correct. If he cheated before, it is quite possible that he would cheat again.

In evaluating history and past relationships, you must also look at yourself. Were you deceived by a previous partner, and did you carry distrust and suspicion into your present relationship? Living through betrayal may have made you more aware—or it may have created a state of constant paranoia in which you think that there is another woman hiding around every corner. When you live in this mental state, you invent your own reality. It is as if you lost a quarter in one pay phone, and now go around expecting every pay phone in town to swallow your change. While this reaction may be understandable, it is unhealthy and certainly not smart behavior. In essence, it is necessary for you to take a step back, look at yourself, and consider the possibility that the problem actually lies within your own psyche.

EVALUATING RECENT EVENTS

Just as you want to evaluate the past, you also want to examine what has recently been going on in both of your lives. Often, sudden changes in routine can cause a mate to go into a tailspin. In both my personal and professional experience, I have noticed that women seem to adapt more readily than men to changes in lifestyle. Changes that affect the intimacy of a relationship or alter the desired level of commitment can be found both inside and outside the home. For example, perhaps there is a new baby in the house causing your attention to be divided. Even the most secure man craves the nurturing provided by a woman. Once, he may have been your moon and stars, but now he may simply be the one who coughs too loudly while the baby is trying to sleep. Nothing overtakes and engulfs a woman like the love for her new baby. As a result, your mate, with his insatiable need to be needed, may desire once again to be the center of someone's universe—and, unfortunately, it may not be yours.

Another area to examine is your mate's career or work situation. Men tend to be at their best when their career is going smoothly. Perhaps his career is not progressing the way he had hoped, or maybe he continues to find himself stuck in a dead-end job. Perhaps, too, your career is moving along at such a pace that he feels threatened or insecure due to your financial independence. This can cause a man to question his importance in your life. It is often during these times, when men find themselves falling short of their personal expectations, that they try to prove themselves through their sexuality.

What all this boils down to is whether your mate feels that he is "the man." If not, he may be a prime candidate for a little extracurricular activity. Therefore it is necessary to evaluate where your partner is in his personal development and professional life compared with where you are, and compared with where he would like himself to be. If the equation is unbalanced and he appears to be falling well short of his expectations, your relationship may be headed for serious trouble.

NOTING CHANGES IN ROUTINE

Next, you'll want to focus on your mate's usual patterns of behavior. Note whether he has begun to change his usual routine, and whether any new behavior is becoming more frequent.

The following are questions that you should ask yourself to assess the way your mate has been acting. When reading these questions, note that some are relevant only if you live together; some, only if you have separate residences.

❏ Does your mate have some new activity that occurs on the same night every week, and to which you are not invited?

❏ Has he started excluding you from activities that the two of you used to share?

❏ Does he mention people you've never heard of and claim that they were all together somewhere?

❏ Does he answer you promptly when you ask where he's been, or does he hesitate before replying?

❏ Does he return home smelling cleaner than he did when he left? Or, conversely, does he jump into the shower immediately after walking through the front door?

❏ Does he carry an extra set of clothing with him wherever he goes? (Pay particular attention to extra underwear.)

❏ Has he suddenly begun doing his own laundry?

❏ Have you begun to notice articles of his clothing missing, especially underwear or T-shirts?

❏ Does he keep cologne in his car?

❏ Has he suddenly begun carrying gum or breath mints with him?

❑ Does he come up with silly reasons as to why he can't wear his wedding band—it's too tight, it will get dirty, it's too expensive, or he doesn't want to damage it? Does he claim to have lost his band altogether?

❑ Are you no longer permitted to open his mail?

❑ Does he suddenly have new possessions that you know he did not have the money to buy?

❑ Is he experiencing a sudden, unexplained interest in getting in shape, going to the gym, or changing his hairstyle and general appearance?

❑ Has he begun washing his car more frequently?

❑ Has he insisted on putting a business telephone line in your home—one to which only he has access and that rings with unusual frequency during nonbusiness hours?

❑ Has he started leaving his cellular telephone or pager in his car at night?

❑ Is his cellular telephone address book or call log locked?

❑ If he answers the telephone in front of you, does he quickly leave the room and speak in hushed tones or cryptic sentences?

❑ Does he hang up the telephone or switch computer screens as soon as you walk into the room?

❑ Does it take him more than a moment or two to respond when you ask him who he was talking to on the telephone?

❑ Has he been taking an unusually long time to return your pages?

❑ When you call him, does he know it's you within a moment or two of hearing your voice, or does he seem confused?

❑ Do you get an inordinate number of hang-ups on your telephone?

❑ Has he recently acquired a phone card?

❑ Have you ever seen either his home or cellular phone bill, or does he make sure that you never get near it?

❑ Does he constantly erase the telephone numbers on his caller ID box or otherwise prevent you from accessing the last telephone number dialed?

❑ Does he constantly check his voicemail or e-mail messages?

❑ Has he recently changed his computer password or any other entry code for no apparent reason?

❑ Has he begun deleting his computer history or other records that would show the websites he's visited?

❑ Has he set up a new e-mail account using a totally different ID of which you were not informed?

❑ Has your home computer been receiving an abundance of spam from online dating or porn sites?

❑ Is his glove compartment locked?

❑ Has he begun to pick petty fights with you, after which he storms out of the house, remaining away for extended periods of time?

❑ Does he have an unusual number of female friends?

❑ Is his ex-girlfriend or ex-wife among his female friends?

❑ Does his ex-girlfriend or ex-wife still not have a new boyfriend or husband of her own?

❑ Do his friends act uncomfortable or weird around you?

❑ Do several of his friends cheat on their wives and girlfriends?

❑ Do you suddenly find the need to adjust the passenger seat in his car every time you get in?

❑ Does he work more overtime, but still never have any money?

❑ Is he extremely suspicious of you, or does he often accuse you of cheating on him for no apparent reason?

❑ Does he suddenly seem uninterested in sex, or, conversely, is he suddenly interested in experimenting with new sexual techniques?

❑ Does he have an unusual number of "stalkers" or ex-girlfriends who just won't leave him alone?

❑ When you leave items at his home, are they still there when you return, or are they buried behind the clothes in his closet?

❑ Are the photos of you in the same place they've always been in his house, car, or office?

❑ Does he always blame the appearance of strange items in his house or car on some phantom?

❑ Does he discourage you from stopping by his house unannounced?

❑ When you do stop by unannounced, how long does it take him to answer the door?

❑ Does he offer pathetic reasons why he can't spend the night at your place?

❑ Does he have even more pathetic reasons why you can't spend the night at his?

❑ Does he call you at work or when you're away simply to see when you'll be home, but at the same time fail to show interest in having a conversation with you?

❑ Does he seem overly restless or unsettled while at home or at your place?

❑ Did he give you only a pager or cellular phone number, and not his home phone number?

❑ Does he unplug his telephone, refuse to answer it, or turn off the ringer altogether when you are around?

❑ Has he forbidden you from answering his telephone?

❑ Does he keep the volume on his answering machine turned all the way down when you're around?

❑ Does he no longer call you after a certain time each day or on weekends?

❑ Does he fail to answer his telephone for extended periods of time, and later claim that he had fallen asleep and did not hear it ringing, or that the phone had been turned off because the battery was charging?

❑ Have you ever met his mother, or has he neglected to introduce the two of you?

❑ Has his mother been calling you by someone else's name?

If you have answered "yes" to more than a handful of these questions, you might already be in serious trouble. Although there may be valid, legitimate reasons for your mate to have exhibited some of these behaviors, you should still make an effort to recognize and note them as they occur.

Consider, too, if your mate has begun to criticize you in areas that never before presented a problem. Perhaps he is making negative comments regarding your hair, weight, style of dress, or level of education. Suddenly it may appear that nothing you do pleases him—that everything about you is wrong. While you should not take these comments personally, you should consider if he might be comparing you to a new love interest.

A red flag may also come in the form of sudden, excessive gifts given for no apparent reason, or sickeningly sweet notes and messages left on your voicemail. Sometimes, these are signs that he is feeling guilty about what he has been up to. Now, I know you should not look a gift horse in the mouth, but it might be time to follow that horse out into the pasture and see what he's been up to!

STAYING ON YOUR TOES

If you are truly interested in noting any signs of infidelity, it is extremely important that you watch and listen to everything that your mate says and does. For example, if he tells you he is going to a recreational activity, such as a sporting event, be sure to ask him, in a matter-of-fact way, who is playing and with whom he is going. Then, when he returns, make certain to ask who won the game, what the score was, and who the star player was. If it was a local event, you can always check to see if his version of the details was correct.

Similarly, if your mate states that he is going to a specific place, always get addresses and routes of travel. Then, if you can, later verify the address and route. Spot-checking is also quite effective. Find an excuse to call him at his friend's house or at the hotel where he's staying. If you have separate residences, every once in a while "find yourself in the neighborhood" and stop by his house. Then, while you're there, make a mental note of any strange car parked in the area, as you may need this information for future reference. Pop in at the gym to tell him his boss called, or bring dinner by his office when he's working late. Always have an on-call babysitter available at five minute's notice so you can free yourself up to check on him when he thinks you're at home with the kids. Show up at the office party to which you were not invited—or at least park inconspicuously outside. You can even go as far as surprising him while he's out of town on that business retreat.

An essential aspect of keeping on your toes is *listening*. Note that listening and hearing are two different things. *Hearing* is your brain's ability to process or perceive sound, while *listening* involves actively paying attention to that sound. You must not only hear the things your mate says to you, but also listen intently to each and every word spoken. You must then remember these words, writing them down if necessary. You must listen when he says he went to the movies with Kyle, and then remember that statement when two weeks later he tells you that he hasn't seen Kyle in months. You must listen when he says he's going to the gym, and then complains days later about how long it's been since he's worked out. You must listen when he discusses a movie with you that he has apparently seen—but not with you. You must listen when he reminds you of a story he thinks he told you, but obviously related to someone else. You must listen as the name of the new girl at the office creeps into more and more of your conversations with him at home. I know you're thinking that this sounds ridiculous and that no man could be so stupid, but the fact of the matter is that the greater the level of deception in which he's involved, the harder it will be for him to keep his stories straight. Sooner or later, he will slip up!

In addition to listening, you'll want to observe—not just his behavior, but that of everyone around you. Body language, for instance, can serve as a major red flag. For example, when you walk into the room at his office holiday party, how do his coworkers look at you? Do they refuse to make eye contact and avoid you at all costs, or do they look at you with obvious pity, as if you were dying of some dreadful disease? Neither of these is a particularly great response. The first reaction probably indicates that no one wants to be chummy with you for fear you will learn their terrible secret. The second reaction probably stems from fear that your "disease"— man-on-the-prowl-itis—may be spreading, and could potentially infect their mates, as well. Note, too, if there is one woman in particular who avoids you like the plague. Be especially concerned if this woman's name has been brought up at home on far too many occasions!

Also be on the alert when in the company of your mate, his friends, and their girlfriends or wives. Do his friends' girlfriends or wives give you that pitiful, sympathetic look? Is there a single female who seems to hang around the group, and appears to be friendly with everyone except you? How does your mate interact with this fifth wheel? Does everyone discuss events and activities in which they all seem to have participated, but from which you were excluded? In other words, when you are in social gatherings, do you get the feeling that everyone knows something you don't? If you have received this impression more than a few times, your worst fears may be valid.

Finally, if you suspect that your mate is cheating but have not yet seen any conclusive signs of these activities, it may be a good idea to observe and keep a mental note of the distance between the various places your mate frequents and the mileage on his odometer. You may even want to drive several routes yourself to establish how many miles and how much time it takes to get from one place to the other. Then, when he says that he drove his buddies to such and such a place last weekend, but his odometer shows only the mileage for a trip to his ex-girlfriend's house and back, you can be sure that something fishy is going on.

KEEPING A MENTAL FILE

The mental file is one of the most important organizational tools you'll employ during your search for the truth. The ability to separate, prioritize, and organize observations and events in your mind is of monumental importance. Your goal is to construct a tight, organized case against your mate. As you are building your case, your mental file will serve as a storage place for all the information you collect. One of the biggest mistakes you can make is to divulge

The Bonus of Staying on Your Toes

On page 14, I explain that by staying alert to your mate's words and actions, you can make yourself more aware of any signs of infidelity. But what if you are more interested in *deterring* your mate from being unfaithful than you are in *catching* him? If that is the case, you'll want to not only stay on your toes, but also make him aware that you're staying on your toes.

Remember that recreational activity your mate was planning to attend on page 14? In addition to asking your partner for the details of the event, before he departs, mention that one of your girlfriends is going to be there and that he should be sure to say "Hi" if he runs into her. This may make him rethink any plans he has to meet another woman, as he will see that you're watching his actions. Similarly, if you ask the details of his intended driving route, even if you have no intention of checking up on him, he may fear that you will and curtail any plans for a rendezvous.

If you choose to use the above tactics to discourage your mate from cheating, I must impress upon you that one of the worst mistakes you can make is to allow him to think that you're "asleep," or that your own behavior is sedentary and predictable. If you show yourself to be unpredictable and inclined to call or show up any place at any time, he may determine that deception takes too much energy and poses too great a risk, and may decide to reserve his cheating nature for a woman who prefers to be asleep.

your information to your mate before you have gathered all the facts you need, as this may cause him to be more clever in his deceptions. As difficult as it may seem to hold onto substantial, incriminating evidence, your entire case may be lost if you don't. You've got to hold on!

At this point, you may be questioning why this information has to be kept in your head, rather than a notebook or file cabinet. Well, it doesn't. You can write down the file information if necessary—*if* you are able to keep it in a place to which your mate will never gain access. But it's far better to maintain a mental file—a file that your mate will never find.

The key to organizing your evidence is the creation of two separate and distinct mental files. The first file we will call *Unsolved Mysteries*; the second, *Bona Fide Horsecrap*. Let's start with the *Unsolved Mysteries* file. In this file, you'll want to store all the stories that seem suspicious but have not yet been proven to be untrue. For example, suppose your mate tells you that he went to the movies with a bunch of friends, but you find only two ticket stubs in his jacket pocket. Now, he may have held onto just two tickets, but still have gone with a bunch of his buddies. At this point, you simply can't be sure. This incident would be filed under *Unsolved Mysteries*. As another example, let's say that your mate claims that he was out all day with his good friend Benjamin, but when he returns home in the evening, he talks to Benjamin on the telephone in a manner which suggests they have not seen each other for quite some time. Now, he and Benjamin may not have discussed the things earlier in the day that you now overhear them discussing on the telephone. So this incident also fits comfortably in the *Unsolved Mysteries* file. The closer you get to uncovering your mate's game, the more of those *Unsolved Mysteries* will begin to make sense to you.

The second mental file, affectionately known as the *Bona Fide Horsecrap* file, is the most difficult file to keep to yourself. This is because it is so full of obvious lies and deceptions that you probably *want* to point out to your mate. This file is reserved for those moments when you call him at work on the night shift and his boss says he isn't at work, and he later claims to have slept in his car all night listening to music. No, you did not see his car and can't say for sure that he wasn't sleeping inside it, but you also know that you are not the village idiot. Therefore, into the *Bona Fide Horsecrap* file it goes.

Creating these mental files serves two main purposes. First, it allows you to organize and build your case. Second, it keeps you from obsessing over and constantly re-evaluating statements and actions that seem suspicious—or worse than suspicious. Once you have filed these things away, it will not be as if they were forgotten; they will simply be reserved for the day you choose to play your hand. In the meantime, though, you'll be able to let them go.

At this point, I'll bet that, once again, you're evaluating whether any relationship is worth this much mental and physical energy. You may already have seen so many red flags that you have decided to end your search for the truth. If that is the case, I wish you well. Then again, you may have decided to ignore any signs of indiscretion and continue with your relationship as if nothing suspect ever happened. Again, I hope you'll be happy with the road you have chosen to travel. However, you may be unable to ignore all signs of infidelity, but still not be absolutely convinced that your mate has betrayed you. If this last perspective describes your own feelings, there is no turning back, for you know too much to rest and too little to give up. So put on your Sherlock Holmes hat, and let's begin building our case.

CHAPTER 2

Gathering the Evidence

In Chapter 1, you learned how to recognize and "file" any signs that your mate is being unfaithful to you. The very fact that you're reading this chapter probably means that you have "smelled a rat." If so, it's time to start gathering physical evidence of your partner's infidelity. This chapter will tell you where to look, when to look, what to look for, how to cover your tracks so that your partner doesn't catch on to what you're doing, and finally, when to stop your search.

At this point—before you begin the hunt for clues—it's important to pause for a moment or two and assess your mental and physical state. You may already be feeling a little shaky as the result of your suspicions. So now, ask yourself if you will be able to handle the results of your efforts. If you think that any true proof of infidelity will cause you to fall apart, take some time to get the help you need before proceeding with your quest. Ask for support from family and friends or speak to your spiritual advisor. If in the past you have called upon God for strength and guidance, by all means, turn to Him again. If necessary, seek professional therapy. The road that you're about to travel is a rough one, and you'll have to be strong if you want to get to the end in one piece, having reached your goal.

It's important, too, to be mindful that the information-gathering process is not an end in and of itself. You may be lucky, and find that your mate is not being unfaithful. If so, the search ahead will be a wonderful and rewarding experience. On the other hand, the evidence that you uncover may support your worst fears. If that is the case, you will have to decide exactly what you want to do with what you find. Unfortunately, you will not be able to uncover information and then forget about it, as if you'd never found it. Instead, you will be left with two choices: You can either use the evidence to show your mate that you're on to his game and that he'd better shape up, or you can take this as an opportunity to leave the relationship. Your ultimate goal will, of course, have no bearing on the techniques you'll be using to gather information. Nevertheless, it is always important to keep your objective in mind as you go about your investigation.

WHEN TO LOOK

Before you begin gathering evidence, it's vital to know *when* you should perform your searches. If you are going to have success, you must pick times when you are in no danger of being interrupted or caught. Your initial searches should be complete, thorough, and tedious, leaving no stone unturned. Then, as you begin building your case, you will learn the art of the thirty-second search.

The best time to conduct a search is when your mate is out of town or occupied in such a way that you have ample opportunity to tear everything apart *and put it back together again*. Safe times include when he's taking a final exam for school, when he is at work, when he is visiting his parents, when he is out of town, and when he is having dental work performed. I can't overemphasize the fact that you should never assume that he is at work, out of town, etc., without verifying it through a phone call or other means. If possible, employ help from friends or family members, who can call you when he is on his way home. You want to be 100-percent certain that you will not get caught.

As mentioned earlier, as you become more efficient in your search, or when you know exactly what you're looking for and can home in on it quickly, you will learn how to perform the thirty-second search. This type of search works best when he leaves his wallet in the car and goes to use the gas station men's room, or when he leaves his coat or pants on the bed and jumps into the shower. This will allow you time to quickly snoop for telephone numbers, receipts, ticket stubs, and any other incriminating evidence. This is also an opportune moment to see if your pictures are still displayed proudly in his wallet. The key to this type of search is to get in and out as quickly as possible.

Before we leave this subject, please understand that you must not be caught snooping! Not only will you look silly, but once your mate learns that you are watching his actions and searching his possessions, he will do a better job of concealing evidence. Therefore, getting caught could be a major setback. Later in this chapter, we will discuss ways to cover yourself if you should happen to get caught nosing around.

WHERE TO LOOK

Where should you look for evidence of your partner's infidelity? The key is to search any area over which your mate has, or believes he has, sole dominion or control. Good places include wallets, especially between credit cards and behind photos; coat pockets; pants pockets, especially that little coin compartment; briefcases; gym bags; day planners; palm pilots; computers; voicemail; pagers; cellular phones; the bottom of dresser drawers; home and cellular phone bills; bank statements; school notebooks and textbooks; nightstand drawers; desks, both at home and in the office, but especially in the office; backpacks; golf bags; CD and audiocassette cases; framed pictures (look behind the frames); pockets of clothing that's hung way in the back of the closet; and garbage cans and wastepaper baskets; as well as various places in his car where things can be stashed—the glove compartment, the trunk, the space under the seats, the sun visors, etc. True, some of these places may be difficult to search, especially if you don't live together. But later in this chapter, you will find tips for gaining access to areas where you feel he could be hiding something.

Above, I mention looking through the pockets of clothing. Be aware, though, that a good deal of evidence can often be found by searching not only clothing pockets, but also the *clothing fabric itself*. Caps, hairbrushes, pillowcases, bed sheets, car head rests, dryer lint screens, bathroom floors, showers, and sinks are also common sources of great clues. What can you find in a lint screen? Later in this chapter, I will detail the treasures that these places harbor.

If you have become suspicious about your mate's Internet activities, you'll also want to check his computer for e-mail, downloaded photos, and other evidence. In some cases, you may even want to use spy software, which can secretly monitor and record all use of the computer, and even send you reports. You can learn more about this in the inset on page 32.

WHAT TO LOOK FOR

You have picked the perfect time and place for your search. But before you actually start your investigation, I want to remind you that all evidence gathered should be placed in the mental files discussed in the previous chapter. (See pages 16 to 19.) As difficult as it may be to hold onto what you consider blatant, undeniable evidence of infidelity, you must understand that moving toward confrontation too quickly could jeopardize your investigation and render all your efforts worthless. You must remain pokerfaced and not reveal your hand until the time is right.

Now you'll want to determine exactly *what* you should be looking for. In general, you should look for anything of any nature that can support your suspicion of infidelity. But over the years, I have found that most clues belong in one of the following categories: slips of paper, including bills, photos, and letters; cell phone information; gifts and keepsakes; clothing; and hair.

Paper

If you followed my advice in Chapter 1, you have been asking your mate specific questions about his activities and carefully noting everything he says. A good way to start your search, then, is to check out the information he's been giving you. For example, if he claims he went to the movies by himself, you will want to see if you can find more than one ticket stub in his possession. If he claims that he's been out of town—or, on the other hand, that he's spent every moment in the office—you'll want to look for gas receipts that state where and when the gasoline was purchased. The most valuable pieces of evidence are often found on the smallest pieces of paper.

Let's say that you come across a slip of paper bearing a mysterious telephone number. First, look at the handwriting. Is it your mate's? Does it look like the handwriting of a woman? Of course, at the first opportunity, you will want to dial the number from a "safe" phone—a phone that would not be recognized by someone who has caller ID. If you are not able to get through to the person, though, don't worry. There are numerous reverse telephone directory websites that will enable you to input a telephone number, and—sometimes for a fee, and sometimes for free—receive the person's name and address. (See Resources on page 85.) Several sites even provide information about cellular telephone numbers, unlisted numbers, and disconnected telephone numbers. These will cost you, but if you are interested in finding the name associated with the phone number in your partner's briefcase, it might be worth the money. Should you pay to track down every number you find among your mate's belongings? Absolutely not. But if these bits of paper as well as your partner's phone records all point to the same unexplained number, you might want to spend the money.

In order to be thorough, you will need to look at every single scrap of paper your mate has in his possession. As already mentioned, the smallest pieces of information often yield the biggest breaks. Furthermore, it's the small things that he is more likely to overlook when destroying evidence. Sometimes, just the fact that your mate found the need to hide something that seems insignificant can be a red flag. For example, if you find that he has hidden the telephone bill, you'll want to take out your calendar and review it with a fine-toothed comb. The telephone bill can yield a wealth of information. Be certain to match up whatever stray telephone numbers you found in his pockets to the numbers on the bill, noting time, duration, and frequency of calls. Neither long nor short calls should be overlooked, as the former may signal that your mate is having more than an occasional chit-chat, while the latter may mean that he is calling simply to say, "I'm on my way over." Also, be certain to take note of calls made to business establishments. My friend once found the number of a pregnancy clinic on her mate's telephone bill—when my friend wasn't pregnant.

Perhaps the most important slips of paper are your mate's credit card bills and bank statements. Believe it or not, some men have been known to use their credit cards to purchase lingerie for which their mate was not the recipient or to rent motel rooms for times when they were supposed to be in the office. A clue may also be found in something as small as the location of an ATM withdraw-al. Perhaps the ATM was located somewhere he had no business being. Or perhaps a large withdrawal was made around the time of his ex-wife's birthday. In that instance, misconduct may be hard to prove, but the information is certainly worthy of being tucked away in your *Unsolved Mysteries* mental file.

When reviewing your mate's bills, pay extremely close atten-tion not only to where and when purchases were made, but also to the amount of the purchase. For example, if he claims that he ate by himself every night of the convention, a food charge of $90 should raise a big red flag. Basically, you want to examine any and all cred-it card bills and bank statements for anything strange, atypical, or in conflict with what he has told you about his activities.

Cell Phones

Cell phones are another great source of evidence. Again, pay atten-tion to even the smallest details. A red light should come on, for instance, when your guy chooses to keep his cell phone unlocked, but regularly locks his address book and call logs. A person who does this is not interested in locking his phone so others can't use it in the event that it is lost. Instead, he is trying to keep his day-to-day communications a secret. If, by chance, you are able to access his cell phone address book, it might provide valuable clues as to what's going on in his life. Pay particular attention to recent, unfamiliar entries. When starting a new relationship, cheaters and noncheaters alike usually find it difficult to memorize a person's home and cel-lular telephone numbers immediately. Although it is highly unlike-ly that the name of your mate's new honey would be fully spelled out and available for your viewing pleasure, it is very possible that her number has been entered in a way that conceals her true identi-ty. For example, the name "LeeAnn" may appear simply as "Lee," giving the impression that the number belongs to a male acquaintance. Or perhaps the name "Julie" might simply appear as "Jay" or "JR." Even if your guy is a social butterfly who is always making new friends, it might not be a bad idea to jot down a few of these new additions to his telephone book, dial them up, and see who answers. You'll want to pay special attention to long distance numbers. If your Internet reverse directory search turns up an address or city in which your mate has no friends, relatives, or business contacts, this could indicate a new online buddy or a recent "acquaintance" he met at that convention he attended last month.

Gifts and Keepsakes

Some men unwisely hold onto cards and letters from their new girlfriend, and even pictures of her or of the two of them together. Usually a man who defines himself as the object of a woman's worship has a difficult time letting go of such keepsakes and love memorabilia, even at the risk of having such items discovered. You may even find gifts that could only have come from another woman. When you discover such undeniable evidence of your mate's indiscretions, keep in mind that the other woman is usually more eager for his game to be exposed than you are. If her goal is to sabotage your relationship and take away your partner, she is apt to leave a trail for you to follow, including detailed letters and dated pictures carefully placed so that you will stumble across them. She will also go out of her way to let you know that another woman has been there. Always be alert and receptive to these clues and keep your eyes wide open; remember, the best evidence can often be found in the simplest places.

Clothing

As previously discussed, your mate's clothing can be a rich resource of evidence. Oh, what experts our noses can become in tracking a rat! Start by doing random "smell checks" of your mate's clothing. This will familiarize you with the routine smell of his clothing. Familiarize yourself, too, with the scent of his cologne, soap, deodorant, and detergent brands, and learn to recognize them in an instant. This will enable you to detect any "foreign" scents—the smell of another woman's detergent or of a motel room soap, for instance. And if you can't readily recognize your own scents—your deodorant and perfume—learn to do so quickly, so that you can distinguish your odors from somebody else's.

Although the odors of perfumes and other toiletry items are the most common scents you'll find on your mate's clothing, you'll also want to take note of other odors, such as those of smoke, pets, and food. Although the smell of tobacco on a nonsmoker's coat or jacket can result from the most innocent of situations, these scents are not as easily explained away when they are present on undergarments. Yes, I am suggesting that you smell your mate's dirty underwear! As disgusting as this may sound, you need to go the entire distance if you want to reach your goal, and dirty underwear can be an excellent source of information! Now, a nonsmoker's underwear will typically smell of smoke only if the wearer has been in the bed of or in close body contact with a smoker. Similarly, underwear will typically smell of perfume only as the result of intimate contact. Dirty T-shirts are much like underwear in the clues that they hold, especially if you're hot on the trail of a foreign perfume.

You'll also want to check your mate's clothes for food smells. After supposedly returning from work, did his shirt have the distinct odor of bacon and eggs? After working late at the office, did his jacket reek of barbecue? If so, take note of the discrepancy and file it away.

Hair

The discovery of hair that undeniably does not belong to you or your mate is valuable indeed. One of hair's greatest attributes is that its fineness and tendency to cling make it so difficult to locate and completely eliminate. The best places to search for hair are the bottoms of your mate's socks, where the hair indicates that he had his shoes off in a foreign place; passenger seat head rests in cars; hairbrushes; bathroom floors; showers; bathroom sinks; bed linen; and dryer lint screens. Always keep an empty envelope with you so that when you spot foreign hairs, you can gather them as quickly as possible. Also remember that darker hairs on darker clothing will most likely be overlooked by the deceiver during his clean-up attempts, as will lighter hairs on lighter clothing.

Once you have gathered the hairs, find a room where you can have some privacy and—using a magnifying glass, if necessary— compare them to some of your own, noting the differences. You will want to observe not only the color and length, but also the texture and ends. (Are they dyed or split?) Keep in mind that hairs on clothing and in cars will be easier for him to explain away than those in bathrooms and bedding. Hair on clothing can be picked up from a chair at work, while that in cars can result from giving a coworker a ride to the train station. Therefore, pay closer attention to those hard-to-explain areas, and always try to gather more than one strand in order to eliminate the possibility that a stray hair followed him home.

After you have gathered sufficient hairs to know that you have a problem, a possible suspect may come to mind. You may recognize that curly blond or straight black hair as being identical to that of a friend, for instance. You may even be able to smell some perfume or tobacco on your "sample." If, however, the foreign hairs fail to suggest a possible suspect, make a mental note to look for a curly blond with black roots—or whatever—among your mate's acquaintances.

Once you have gathered any and all of the physical evidence described above—paper, clothing, hair, etc.—you will need to *secretly* interrogate your mate in order to determine which clues are relevant and which can be adequately explained. Just because the presence of certain items can be explained, however, does not mean that you should discard them. You may be surprised by how many presumably innocent clues ultimately get placed in the *Bona Fide Horsecrap* file! You will need to master inconspicuous interrogation by simply asking roundabout, nonthreatening questions in order to slyly elicit information from your mate. Remember, practice makes perfect!

HOW TO GATHER AND RECORD EVIDENCE

You have already learned when you should conduct a search, where you should perform a search, and what you should look for. But you still need to learn how you can physically gather the evidence and, in some cases, how you can record it for later use. Of course, you can't gather or record the smell found on a dress shirt or certain other clues, but many other types of evidence can be preserved for later examination.

As you might suspect, your method of gathering evidence will vary according to the type of evidence you seek. Some forms of information can be obtained simply by talking to your mate, while other forms must be uncovered through more "scientific" means. Now, by scientific, I don't mean that you have to be a PhD. Every technique required can be easily used by the average person. Moreover, every item that you'll need to help you in this process is either already in your home, or can be easily obtained online or at a neighborhood store.

Before we look at various means of gathering evidence, I'd like to repeat that all of these tasks must be performed secretly, without tipping your hand to your mate. Whenever you conduct a search, you want to make sure that you have both the time and privacy you need to avoid being discovered.

Using Your Computer to Search for Evidence

As discussed on page 24, you may have reason to believe that your mate is using his computer to keep in touch with other women, or that his computer may at least provide some evidence of his extracurricular activities. If so, there are many ways to find what you're looking for.

To begin, you will probably want to search the computer's "History," "Cookies," and temporary Internet files. If the computer's "Auto Complete" option is enabled, you can also perform a cursory search by simply clicking on the "Start" tab at the bottom of the screen, and then on "Search." Start entering letters of the alphabet to see what searches have been conducted on the computer, or use the search function to locate any files, folders, and pictures that have been saved on the computer. One way to find photos is to enter ".jpg" into the search screen, or to check "Programs Files" and run a find file on all .jpgs. You might also check the computer for files such as "getmsg" for old hotmail e-mails, which can also sometimes be found in "Temp Internet Files." Additionally, check his add/remove programs for instant messaging options.

Many people who suspect that their mate is corresponding with love interests online choose to install spy software on their computers. Depending on the exact program used, this software can allow you to secretly monitor and record all of a user's activities, including websites visited, windows opened, Internet chats, e-mails sent and received, and every key pressed. Some programs even take snapshots of the desktop at set intervals. Detailed reports of computer use can be hidden in the machine for later retrieval, or sent to another computer.

Many different types of spy software are available. Spectorsoft's eBlaster, while costly, is preferred by many people not only because of its many spyware capabilities, but also because it allows remote installation and monitoring, and is both undetectable and reliable. Other useful programs include BlazingTools Perfect Keylogger and Keylogger Spy. New programs are always being made available, so I suggest that you perform a search for the latest spy software, visit the websites of the various companies, and, if necessary, contact the companies for more information. You'll then have the data you need to determine the best program for your specific situation.

Be aware that your mate may have installed a program, such as Shredder or Norton Anti-Virus, to notify him if anyone adds spy software. You should therefore run each of these programs to make sure that they didn't spot your installation. Also remember to reboot the machine and run the test message after installing the software. Generally, when a new program is installed, it is inactive until the computer is rebooted, at which point it indicates that new software has been added. You therefore have to reboot both to activate the program and to make sure that when your mate next uses his computer, he does not immediately see a message telling him about the new spy software!

Finally, be aware that spy software is perfectly legal to use as long as you are installing in on a machine that is in your own home.

Copying Paper Evidence

As you find your evidence, one of your most valuable allies will be the copy machine. You will need to check out the area surrounding your mate's home or office to find the closest and most easily accessible machine so that when you locate an important piece of information, you can copy it and return it to its original location in as timely a manner as possible. Let's look at two ways in which this can be handled.

In the first case scenario, you are able to conceal the little goody—the credit card bill, or whatever—on your person, hightail it to your buddy the copy machine, and return the document to its resting place in record time. Now, keep in mind that this option may require your making an "emergency" trip to the drugstore at 2:00 AM in order to buy cough medicine or aspirin, or for some other reason that will enable you to duck out without arousing suspicion. When you return from your mission, it is extremely important that you remember not only to put the original document back exactly where you found it, but also that you stash the copy in a safe place until you have the time and privacy to safely examine it. Please, do not put yourself in a position where you'll have to explain why a copy of your partner's telephone bill was in the pocket of your jacket! And no matter how tempted you may be, *do not* examine the bill until you are in a safe place and absolutely cannot get caught! Until that time, put the copy someplace where your mate will not see it—in an interior zipped compartment of your purse, for instance, or in the trunk of your car.

In the second case scenario, you are not in a position to make copies at the moment of discovery, and must conceal the bill in such a way that you will be able to quickly locate it again on another occasion. Now, by "conceal," I don't mean that you should place the item in a garbage bag under the kitchen sink. You must put it someplace where it will remain safe and, if found, will not arouse suspicion. For example, perhaps you could place the document in a stack of semi-recent newspapers—and maybe offer to take them out to the recycling bin one day—or situate it between some books or magazines that are lying around the living room. If your mate accidentally comes across the slip of paper in its new location, he will probably think that he left it there himself. Only the very cleverest of individuals would ever imagine that you stashed it among his possessions with the idea of later making a photocopy! It is very important, however, to plan on returning and making your copies within about two days of concealment. Don't tempt fate.

Other items that you will want to copy include pay stubs, pages of your partner's personal phone book, cards and letters, photos, ticket stubs, and whatever other documents you feel support your suspicions. Remember that there is no need to take photographs to a photo lab, as basic black-and-white copies will definitely serve your purpose. Once you have secured your copies and moved them to a safe location, you will be able to examine them carefully for the types of information discussed earlier in the chapter.

Gathering Hair

Earlier, I went into great detail regarding the importance of gathering hair from your mate's clothing. Although loose hair is usually quite visible to the naked eye, if your mate is aware that you are looking for it, he may go out of his way to remove each piece from his clothing. Therefore it is important that you do a more thorough search of the material in question in order to locate and collect each and every strand.

First, wrap a couple of strips of clear tape around your fingers with the adhesive side facing outwards. Then, run your fingers lightly across the material in question, back and forth, and see what adheres to the tape. You may be surprised by what you are able to pick up. If you find the tape method to be frustrating or too time-consuming, simply use a lint brush, just as if you were removing lint from your clothing. Once you have finished gathering the hair from all surfaces in question, separate the foreign hair from the lint and place the hair in your ever-handy envelope for future inspection.

Monitoring Phone Calls

We've already discussed how you can locate and copy your mate's phone bills as a means of learning whom he's been calling. Another way of learning the identity of callers is to install a caller ID box, which can display the name and phone number of a caller and, depending on the device, keep a record of the last fifty or more calls received. Because your mate may erase the number on the box that's hooked up to the telephone he generally uses, it's an excellent idea to install a second box in an unused phone jack. This will provide you with your own personal record of all calls that come into the house.

I would be remiss if I failed to discuss the use of tape recorders to record telephone conversations between your mate and whomever he speaks to on the phone. I know of several cases in which a woman purchased a recorder and carefully concealed it near the phone most frequently used by her mate. When the mate received a call, the woman made up an excuse to leave the house, turned on the recorder, and exited the house. In most cases, even if the man being taped had hung the phone up prior to her leaving the house, he quickly returned the call, and the ensuing conversation was recorded. Those women who did this successfully made sure that they were back before the recorder turned itself off with a loud clicking sound, which would have alerted the mate to the device. When not in use, they also took care to store the recorder near the phone, but to conceal it in a briefcase, gym bag, etc. Some even used a voice-activated recorder, so that it could be left on for extended periods of time.

With that said, be aware that in all states, it is *illegal* to tape-record a conversation unless at least one party to the conversation—either the mate or the person to whom he's talking—is aware that he is being taped. In some states, it is actually illegal to tape conversations unless *all* parties are aware of the tape recorder. Anyone caught making a tape without the required knowledge and consent can be prosecuted.

Videotaping Activities Within Your House

Nearly everyone by now has heard of a nanny-cam—a video camera installed in the house to record the activities of a babysitter. Of course, it is also possible to install a video camera to record the activities of your mate so that you will know what he's up to when you're out of the house. With today's technology, small video cams can remain virtually undetectable. Not only can they record activities for later playback, but via e-mail, they can transmit live images while they are operating. I am aware of numerous situations in which these cameras have provided someone with the proof she needed of her mate's infidelity. However, there is some controversy regarding the legality of using these devices, so it would make good sense to check the laws in your state. And I certainly do not advise installing such a device in someone else's home.

ENLISTING HELP IN THE SEARCH

So far, for the most part, I've discussed ways in which you can gather evidence on your own. But sometimes, it's helpful to enlist the help of an ally. Now, this can be tricky. You have to use exceptional judgment when recruiting someone else's assistance, but, if done properly, the benefits can be great.

The best type of ally is someone who may have inside knowledge of your mate's activities but who feels no particular allegiance

A Word About Passwords

I do not condone your obtaining your mate's computer password, voicemail password, or other entry code. However, I can advise you on ways to protect your *own* password from a mate who suspects that you are gathering evidence on his activities, and is therefore interested in monitoring *your* actions.

First of all, keep in mind that most people settle on only one or two letter or number combinations that they use for everything. For example, their ATM pin code, voicemail access code, computer password, and alarm code may all be the last few digits of their social security number, their date of birth, or the name of their pet. Therefore, if you are concerned about someone stealing your password or access code, it would be a good idea to change a digit or two at the end of your code in order to protect your privacy. Also keep in mind that if your mate asks you for your ATM code in order to perform a bank transaction for you, he might then try that same code to access your voicemail or unlock your cell phone.

Also be aware that when telephones store the last number dialed, it is easy for another person to press redial and capture your voicemail passcode. I once knew a man who checked his voicemail messages from his girlfriend's house. The woman was later able to capture his passcode from her redial screen, and subsequently access his voicemail. It therefore pays to be careful when accessing personal accounts from another individual's home or telephone, and to be alert to the person who seems to be encouraging you to access your accounts when you're away from home.

to him. Preferably, this person should have something to gain by sharing information with you, but not to the point that his truthfulness is called into question. Furthermore, this person must be not only willing to help, but also loyal to the point where he would never reveal this alliance to your mate.

Although there are several factors to consider when enlisting the help of an ally, the single most important concept, which I cannot emphasize enough, is that you must *never reveal your sources.* Keep in mind that anyone who helps you to secure information, for whatever reason, is putting himself out on a limb. Once you reveal the identity of your ally, you will probably never, ever have access to that resource again. That person will probably feel betrayed and will deny having told you anything. As a result, your relationship with this person will be destroyed, any current or any future investigation will be destroyed, and this person may even be in danger. That is why you must forever hold onto the names of your sources.

Later on, in Chapter 3, I will discuss ways to present evidence obtained from an ally without revealing its true origin. But as for now, no matter what happens or how desperate you may feel, please, please, please don't ever reveal your sources!

With that caveat in mind, I urge you to start considering the people in your life with an eye towards choosing a collaborator. Then, if no one comes to mind, consider the following candidates.

Your Mate's Best Friend's Wife or Girlfriend

The wife or girlfriend of your mate's best friend probably has the inside track on "guy talk" you may have missed. Certainly, her partner shares information with her about your mate, just as your partner probably tells you about his best friend. She may feel sorry for you if she knows about your partner's infidelity. Or she may feel that birds of a feather should stick together, and question if her husband or boyfriend is involved in the same sort of extracurricular activity. Especially if she is insecure about her own relationship, she may be willing to make a pact with you, agreeing to tell you about your mate if you share information about her guy.

Of course, this alliance is risky, because there is always the chance that she may let her partner know about your suspicions. Therefore, it may be wise to form this partnership only when this woman is suspicious of her own mate, or if she has caught him cheating in the past. In either of these cases, she will probably sympathize with you and be unlikely to undermine your efforts to learn the truth.

Your Mate's Ex-Best Friend or "Close" Enemy

You certainly know what I mean by a best friend. By "close" enemy, I am referring to someone to whom your mate was once very close, but with whom he has had a recent, major falling out. Now, keep in mind that this person may have his own agenda and may embellish the truth in order to settle some score with your mate, but that does not mean that you shouldn't hear what he has to say. Even if only 10 percent of what this person tells you is true, that's 10 percent more than you knew before. The best aspect of enlisting the help of this ally is that you won't have to worry about his telling your mate about your game plan—at least, not for as long as they remain enemies.

Your Mate's Sister or Other Female Relative

Tread carefully here! Blood is certainly thicker than water. However, if you have a good relationship with your partner's family—if they respect you and hate the fact that you're suffering because of his actions—a member of his family might make a good ally. This can work especially well if his sister was a friend of yours prior to your meeting him, or if he and his sister or he and another female relative are not getting along for some reason.

Your Mate's Coworker

A coworker of your mate who is also a friend of yours is another possible candidate. Coworkers are privy to lunchroom chatter, and may even overhear your mate talking on the phone to other women. As such, they can be a valuable source of information. Even if your mate is not so indiscreet that he talks candidly to this coworker, this ally can at least keep you abreast of any workplace gossip. True enough, gossip is merely gossip, but very often, it is founded in at least a partial truth. A coworker can also obtain information from, say, your mate's Rolodex, or gather paperwork that you deem important and that your mate is keeping in the office.

Naturally, a coworker is also a great source of information about your mate's work hours. Has he truly been working overtime on a project? Was he really attending a convention? Plus, the coworker would have information about your mate's secretary—is she really fat and ugly?—and about the other people with whom he's working.

If you choose to form an alliance with one of your mate's coworkers, it is very important that you refrain as much as possible from even mentioning this ally's name to your partner. Once your mate recognizes that you and this coworker have become friends, you can pretty much count on the well of information drying up. It should go without saying, of course, that before entering such an alliance, you should have a complete and accurate understanding of this person's relationship with your mate. You don't want to find that the person you thought was an ally was really the other woman!

Acquaintances

If friends and family members cannot or will not supply you with the information you need, you may want to look beyond them to the many people with whom you and your mate have casual contact either occasionally or on a day-to-day basis. These people—who would serve more as information sources than as allies—include neighbors, barbers, parcel service deliverers, classmates, grocery store clerks, accountants, teachers, secretaries, babysitters, bank tellers, income tax preparers, dry cleaning operators, receptionists, and yes, even ex-girlfriends. Although there is no need to put any of these people through a full interrogation, you may be surprised by the amount of information that can be obtained by posing a seemingly harmless question.

Support Groups

The final group of people who might help you in your search include those who you'd meet through a website geared toward infidelity survivors. (See Resources on page 85.) I am a member of several such sites, and have found the available resources extremely helpful. For example, perhaps you want to make a telephone call in order to check on the whereabouts of your mate. Instead of making the call yourself and risk alerting him to your suspicions, you can enlist the help of another chat group member. Because the folks who join these sites will be sympathetic to your situation, they will probably be more than willing to help out. Whether or not the group members help you search for clues, they will certainly provide a sounding board for your thoughts, or at least a place to vent. Just be sure that when you visit an infidelity survivor website, you erase your tracks in the computer's records and otherwise prevent your mate from discovering that you have been there. As discussed before, you don't want him to know that you're watching him, and thus allow him to stay one step ahead of the game!

All information you gather through allies and acquaintances should, of course, be stored in one of your mental files. Once you have compared your mate's story with the information gathered from these sources, you will be able to determine if your partner's version is either an *Unsolved Mystery* or *Bona Fide Horsecrap*. Even if the story seems to check out, it should be filed away until the conclusion of your investigation.

COVERING YOUR TRACKS

Now that you are in the midst of a full-fledged search for evidence, you must incorporate another important skill into your repertoire. You must perfect the art of covering your tracks—of explaining why you are looking through his wallet, his pockets, or whatever.

Although I have warned you repeatedly to proceed with the utmost of caution, even professionals sometimes get caught in the act of gathering evidence. That is why it is so important to always establish a reason for being where you are *before* you get there! For example, before you get caught looking through your mate's wallet, be prepared to say that you were looking for two fives for the ten *that you already have in your hand*. Before you start searching the floor of his car, be sure to mention the earring that you think you lost there. Then, when he walks up behind you and catches you in his car on all fours, you can say—hopefully, without getting flustered—"Remember the other night when I told you I lost my earring? Well, my sister wants to borrow that pair." The lost earring excuse is, in fact, one that works well in a lot of situations, as when searching bathroom floors and sheets, because an earring is so small that you can pretend to have lost it practically anywhere without arousing suspicion.

Another tactic is to give your mate a letter you want mailed. Then, a couple of days later, when you get caught searching his briefcase, backpack, or coat pocket, you can claim that the letter never arrived and you were checking to see if he remembered to mail it. Are you starting to get the picture? Note that there is no need to make your excuse believable; it's just important to have one. For example, "I'm searching through your laptop because my sister wants to purchase one, and I wanted to tell her which type of system you have." Or, "I wanted to buy you a new computer for your birthday, and I needed to see what type would be compatible with the software you already have." Sound believable? Probably not; but a lot of his stories may be just as ridiculous, so who cares!

Some situations require more creativity than others. For instance, if you get caught examining his telephone bill, you can claim to be questioning why his monthly service charges are so much lower than yours. Or if he catches you scanning his credit card bill, you can claim you were thinking of switching banks, and wanted to compare his finance charges with yours. I'm sure you can come up with a multitude of your own explanations. Just keep in mind that you have to have these lines ready *before* you start snooping so you can deliver them without hesitation.

Before we leave this topic, note that these same techniques may also be helpful later on, when you present your case to your mate. As you will learn in Chapter 3, the first thing your mate will say upon being shown the evidence against him is, "What were you doing snooping through my car?" Believe me when I tell you that it will make things so much easier if you are already prepared with your answer: "I was looking for my earring!" Then you will be able to move on to more important issues.

WHEN TO STOP

One of the most important parts of undertaking this type of hunt is to know when to stop. There comes a time when you must recognize that enough is enough. Although this point may come at a variety of different junctures for different people, it is vital that you realize it, step back, assess, and decide on your next course of action.

The clearest sign that you have reached the end of your search occurs when you realize that you can make an airtight case against your mate. At this point, you will have gleaned information from allies and other informants; confirmed the validity of a large portion of that information through the use of material evidence such as notes, letters, and telephone bills; and perhaps even sealed your case with photos or your own visual observations. Possibly, several of your mate's stories, once classified as *Unsolved Mysteries*, have been transferred to your *Bona Fide Horsecrap* file. Once you have reached this point, there is little or no reason to continue your search. Of course, there is always the possibility that you have gone on a wild goose chase and that your mate was *not* doing anything wrong. If that is the case, congratulations! Be aware, though, that the very fact that you felt the need to investigate your mate indicates a problem in the relationship. By all means, consider counseling.

Another indication that it's time to stop comes when you become so engrossed in your search that you cannot concentrate on anything else. You may, for instance, get so involved in collecting evidence that you are unable to eat or sleep, to carry on daily activities of living, or to sustain a single thought that is not related to finding proof of your mate's infidelity. You may begin to follow every car that resembles the car of the suspected lover, to constantly call her house and hang up, or to search the same places over and over again, looking for what you may have already found. When this happens, do not continue your search!

Some people find it difficult to stop gathering evidence because the thrill of the search provides an adrenaline rush. However, continuing to investigate every single word, story, and stray telephone number is not only unnecessary, but also self-destructive. As important as it is to avoid ending your search prematurely, it is equally important to avoid obsessing over facts that have already been confirmed. For example, once you've driven by the new woman's house and seen his car parked outside, it is not necessary to drive by every day. Once you have found photos and love letters, it is not necessary to keep searching for hairs. It's time to let it go! This extra energy can be put to more positive use by developing your next plan of action. Be aware, too, that there will be some pieces of evidence that will *never* make sense and will never fit into the puzzle. But as long as you've already collected sufficient evidence, there is no need to place every piece of the puzzle. You already have the picture.

For most people, the conclusion of the search, rather than bringing a sigh of relief, is a difficult and confusing time. You may now be forced to deal with the reality of your relationship. You may even begin to wish that you had never undertaken the search in the first place. But as difficult as it may seem, you need to hold yourself together for just a little while longer and start planning your confrontation. That's what Chapter 3 is all about. It will guide you in reassessing your ultimate goal, and help you decide when, where, and how you will present the evidence you have gathered to your mate.

CHAPTER 3

Confrontation

Well, you've done it! You have put lots of time and effort into your investigative work and feel certain that the evidence you've found points to an unfaithful partner. Hopefully you've been able to maintain a reasonable level of mental stability (and haven't gotten yourself committed or incarcerated) because you are going to need a lot of strength to get through the next phase—the confrontation.

This is likely to be a bittersweet time for you. Although you may feel a certain sense of satisfaction resulting from your hard work and perseverance, what you have uncovered will undoubtedly prompt feelings of anger or sadness. For some of you, the search may have been relatively easy; for others, it may have been a seemingly endless ordeal rife with mental, physical, and emotional stress. No matter how you got to this point, it is time to take a step back and reassess your purpose for gathering the evidence in the first place. Then you have to establish a game plan.

REASSESS YOUR GOALS

Do you believe that your relationship is worth salvaging? This is an important question that you must honestly answer before you arrange a confrontation with your mate. Are you really ready to let go, or do you just want to present your partner with enough evidence to make him aware that you're on to him and that he'd better shape up? In either case, you will have to be very careful about the type of evidence you present and about how much of it you choose to disclose.

So often a cheater will attempt to bait you into that old game of "Tell me all the evidence you have against me before I admit to anything." During this game, the cheater evaluates the strength of your case before deciding whether or not he really needs to come clean. Don't fall for it! Whether you plan to give him another chance or not, do not ever reveal more than a few fragments of information. For example, you might want to tell him that two movie tickets "fell out" of his coat pocket, but don't tell him there were far too many miles on his odometer for him to have simply gone to the gym and back. Or you might say that you found the letter from his ex, but don't let him know that you found her number repeated over and over again on his phone bill.

Another rationale for holding back bits of evidence is that, in the event you choose to give him another chance and continue the relationship, retaining some of your tricks and tactics will enable you to check up on him in the future. It is okay for him to believe that you looked through his pockets (he probably knew that anyway), but it is not wise to alert him to the video camera you used to document his bedroom antics. (Once he knows about that one, rest assured, he will never let it happen again!) Keep a few investigative techniques up your sleeve. This way, in the future, you can see whether or not he has gotten his act together and changed his ways, or if he is up to the same old tricks!

Even if you plan to tell your mate to hit the road—that there is no second chance—it is still unwise to divulge all of your evidence. Just give him the bare minimum. There is a good chance that he may defend himself with more lies, crying about how what you have uncovered was only a "one-time fling" and that "she didn't mean anything" to him. He might claim that the "other woman" was the one pursuing him and he was simply the victim of a stalker. Or he may try to convince you that she had initially liked one of his buddies, and that he got stuck in the middle as an innocent go-between. While you are listening to his lies, you will know the truth. The evidence you have not shared with him—you have a copy of his cell phone bill with over fifty calls to her house, you found some of her hair fragments in his shower, or you've heard the "friendly" messages she left on his voicemail—will give you the strength and confidence to walk out the door . . . and know you are making the right decision.

Another reason to keep some of your evidence under wraps is to prevent the guilty party from turning the tables and putting you in a defensive position. This is a common tactic in which the one caught cheating becomes the indignant accuser, making you defend how and why you were where you were to get what you got. Later in this chapter, we will explore ways to recognize and handle these situations in a section called "Jedi Mind Games." (See page 55.) Finally, if you spill your entire bag of tricks, your cheating partner is sure to alert his friends so that they, too, can be on the lookout for these same tactics from their girlfriends or wives.

Never give up too much evidence. I cannot stress this point enough. Let him speculate over the sources of your information; let him wonder if you've hired a private investigator.

WHEN, WHERE, AND HOW

Once you have decided what you want from your confrontation—

whether it is to give him "another try" or to simply "say good-bye"—it is time to determine the most productive way to proceed.

Whatever your plan, try to avoid going into a ranting, raving, screaming fit as he walks through the front door. Not only is this an ineffective approach, but it is also emotionally and physically draining. Think about it. Picture yourself standing there screaming accusations at him, and then watch as he turns around and walks back out the door. Now what? There you are, with all of your evidence ready and waiting to go, acting like a crazed person who has become emotionally unhinged. An important part of your confrontation is being able to take note of and evaluate his responses and body language as you present bits of evidence. This is impossible to accomplish when you are screaming, yelling, and throwing things—not a good plan.

When preparing for your confrontation, it is also important to know the kind of person you are dealing with. When cornered, is he the type who is likely to become enraged and possibly threaten you with physical violence? If so, you don't need this book to give you a reason to end the relationship. Is he the type who tends to raise his voice and create a scene? If this is a likely reaction, be sure to choose your venue wisely. Although you may desire the security of confronting your partner in a public place such as a restaurant, you may not want to face the embarrassment of a screaming match. Or is he is the kind of guy who is likely to show instant guilt and remorse, perhaps even shed a tear or two? If this seems like a possibility, stay strong and maintain your focus—and be sure to keep a tissue box handy!

The art of a truly effective confrontation lies in knowing that you have gathered more than enough facts to prove your case, and you have arranged them in a logical, sometimes chronological, order. When I say enough evidence to "prove" your case, I do not mean that you have to prove the case to your mate. I mean you have to prove it to yourself.

It is important to have more than one bit of evidence to support your belief. Granted, finding a letter from the new office intern tucked in the bottom of his sock drawer that gushes "I can't stop thinking about those nights we lay holding each other and making incredible love," may certainly seem like proof enough—but don't jump the gun. You see, in order to have a successful confrontation, this letter should really be combined with further evidence. For instance, in addition to the letter, you've found one or two of his T-shirts that bear the faint aroma of perfume that is definitely not your brand, and long strands of blond hair keep appearing on the passenger seat of his car. I have known of many cases in which women have immediately confronted their partners at the first sign of infidelity, whether it was a letter, a motel receipt, or a perfume-scented article of clothing. In a number of these instances, the cheating spouses were clever enough to quickly spin elaborate tales that explained away the glaring bit of evidence. I have even known of one guy who claimed he was being "set up." Eventually, however, the truth comes out—usually with the surfacing of additional evidence. So try to control any impulses to make immediate accusations. It is always better to first gather enough facts that prove (to you) your partner's infidelity.

As with any crime, the most effective way of determining the truth—the ideal manner of confrontation—is to catch the suspect in the act. Although facing this type of reality is, without a doubt, most effectual, it is also very painful. But if you are the type who is willing, able, and strong enough to catch your unfaithful partner red-handed, there are some strategies you can follow to implement such a plan.

Remember, there is nothing more accurate and telling than the element of surprise. Let's say, for example, you discover that on Friday mornings, shortly after you leave for work, your partner has "company." Take the day off, and return to the house unexpectedly. Talk about a wake-up call! Under such a circumstance, there is no need to present any other backup evidence; the moment will speak for itself. Or if you know that the unsuspecting couple has planned to meet at an out-of-the-way motel or will be spending the weekend together under the guise of a "company seminar," follow them to their destination. Once they are tucked away in their room, hold your breath until the lights go out and then, surprise! I think you get the picture. There's probably a great story behind the line, "He got caught with his pants down."

I know a woman who followed her husband to his mistress's apartment. She waited outside the door and listened for a moment of silence within the apartment. After knocking, she slipped a note under the door, asking the mistress to send her husband down when she was finished with him. The wife then went to the parking lot, and waited for her husband in his car. Believe me, there was nothing he could say!

If you are not afforded the opportunity to stage your plan and catch him in the act, you can implement the next best strategy—catching him in a lie. This means waiting for the right time, a time when you are certain that he is lying about his whereabouts. Like the night he claims he is at the gym with Fred, but Fred has already called twice that evening looking for him. You also have evidence that supports the fact he has been seeing another woman on his so-called "gym nights" for the past few months. When he comes home, by implementing the right dialogue, you can catch him in a lie. The following conversation serves as an example:

ANGEL: How was the gym?

DEVIL: Fine.

ANGEL: I drove by and didn't see your car.

DEVIL: I rode with Fred.

ANGEL: I went into the gym and you weren't there. (Keep in mind, you never actually left home.)

DEVIL: I left early.

ANGEL: Do you always leave early?

DEVIL: No, just tonight, why?

ANGEL: Oh, because I *always* drive by the gym, and your car is *never* there, and you are *never* inside, and Fred *always* calls here looking for you. So, last week I decided to follow you . . . and guess what I discovered . . .

Get the picture? Even though you may never have actually followed him (you may have simply heard her voicemail messages, or one of your allies may have tipped you off), you have still caught him red-handed in the middle of a lie. And rest assured, more will follow!

Another strategy for catching your partner in a lie is to start out with some innocent-sounding questions before hitting him between the eyes with the serious ones. For instance, you have discovered that your husband is seeing someone he works with, and that they get together every Tuesday night. When he walks through the door late one Tuesday night, it would be strategic to begin the conversation like:

ANGEL: (sympathetically) Boy, you must be exhausted after putting in such a long day at work.

DEVIL: (comfortably) Yeah, it's been tough trying to get that project finished before the deadline.

ANGEL: By the way, who is Jenny, and how many more Tuesday nights are you going to pretend to be working late while you're really out with her?

The strategy here is to put him at ease and catch him in the first lie before coming out with your facts. If you start off with an accusatory, "Where were you tonight?" he will know you are on to something and immediately try to cover his tracks. It's much better to maintain your cool and allow him to feel comfortable while you are setting him up. In other words, don't let him see you coming.

It is always a good practice to ask questions for which you already have the answers. Let's say that after you confront your husband regarding his affair with Jenny, he seems sincerely sorry and promises to break it off. A few months later, however, the signs of infidelity, along with incriminating evidence, begin to reappear. When the time is right, you once again confront your husband:

ANGEL: (casually, innocently) Do you still talk to Jenny?

DEVIL: Nope. Not at all.

ANGEL: Do you think she still loves you?

DEVIL: How the heck would I know? Like I said before, I never talk to her.

ANGEL: Then what are all those letters about, and why were they hidden in your glove compartment?

Of course, he might come up with the "She's a stalker" routine, but you have already done your homework and know the truth. You have seen his car parked around the corner from her house numerous times in the past few weeks, and her telephone number has appeared on his cell-phone bill over and over and over . . .

Yes, it is certainly important to build a good strong case before confronting your unfaithful partner. As tempting as it may be to take your first piece of evidence and run into battle, it is not strategically sound. Doing so would only give him the opportunity to talk his way out of trouble. He might be able to easily explain why his car was parked in front of her house all night ("It broke down there and I walked to a gas station"); but it would be much more difficult to *also* explain why her mail was found in his car, or why there was such a large restaurant bill charged to his Visa card on her birthday.

JEDI MIND GAMES

Have you ever been in a situation in which you had all of the facts and were ready to wage war, but once the confrontation began, you found yourself on the defensive? Things became so confused and convoluted that somehow, within a matter of seconds, you were the one under attack, struggling to justify your actions. What you experienced, or more appropriately, "fell victim to," is what I affectionately refer to as a *Jedi mind game.*

Jedi mind games are played so quickly, you hardly know what hit you. You may start off waging a justified war, but end up apologizing to the villain. And as you walk away, you'll probably be asking yourself, "Now how in the world did that happen?" Well, I am here to tell you that you have been a victim of one of the oldest tricks in the book. Here's a sample conversation that takes place during a classic Jedi mind game:

ANGEL: I found this used condom in your garbage can!

DEVIL: So what are you saying, it's supposed to be mine?

ANGEL: You're the only one who lives here!

DEVIL: So what? You know Tom, Dick, and Harry are over here all the time! Oh, so now you're searching through my garbage cans? What the hell's the matter with you? You don't trust me? (an exasperated sigh) You know, you and your little insecurities are really beginning to get on my nerves! Talk about paranoia! You've got some real problems! You know, I can't live like this . . . I don't think this is going to work!

And before you know it, you find yourself on the defensive and apologizing to him.

One of the best ways to avoid becoming a victim of this type of mind game is to open your eyes and be aware of its identifying features, of which there are several. For starters, in a typical Jedi mind game, before the issue you have raised has been addressed, you will find yourself immediately under attack. This is a classic attempt to buy some time until he can come up with some sort of explanation. During the confrontation, you are also likely to be accused of being someone who is possessive, insecure, crazy, psycho, sneaky, looking for trouble, controlling, immature, trying to start something, and just like his ex-girlfriend—all before you get an adequate explanation for the evidence you have presented. These tactics, which throw you to the left while he escapes to the right, often work with amazing success. As soon as the question of why another woman's black lace panties are stuck under the sheets at the foot of his bed turns into a personal attack on your character and mental stability, you are in the middle of a Jedi mind game. Don't fall prey to it!

The best way to avoid these tricks is to steer clear of them in the first place. As you learned in the last chapter, remember to always have a reason for being where you were when you found what you found. This will help you to avoid the "Why were you looking in my coat pocket?" counterattack. Try to arrange the facts of your confrontation in such a way that the information obtained just sort of "accidentally" landed in your lap. If you can, avoid having to confess that you were snooping.

Another way to avoid a Jedi mind game is to always have numerous pieces of information on hand. Then when he tries to attack you or downplay the validity of the first bit of evidence, you can hit him with another and another until he crumbles under your successive blows. As you will discover, although it may be easy for him to dispute one piece of evidence, it will be far more difficult to explain away a series of incriminating facts.

If you find yourself being baited into a Jedi mind game, try to turn the tables on him. Hit him with a line such as "You still haven't answered the question," "Do you really think I'm that stupid?" "Don't try to turn it around!" or "Nice try. What movie did you get that story from?" Using the right line at the right time will deflect the severity of his attack by placing the focus back where it belongs—on him and his pitifully weak excuses. By way of example, consider the following:

ANGEL: I found this used condom in your garbage can!

DEVIL: So what are you saying, it's supposed to be mine?

ANGEL: You're the only one who lives here!

DEVIL: So what? You know Tom, Dick, and Harry are over here all the time! Oh, so now you're searching through my garbage cans?

ANGEL: Look, I noticed it was full, so I decided to empty it.

DEVIL: What the hell's the matter with you? You don't trust me?

ANGEL: Stop trying to turn it around and answer the question! Where did the condom come from?

DEVIL: You know, you and your little insecurities are really beginning to get on my nerves!

ANGEL: I'm still waiting for an answer . . . and while you're at it, you can also tell me who the blond is, and where you go on Friday nights when you're supposed to be working late!

DEVIL: Talk about paranoia! You've got some real problems!

ANGEL: Do you really think I'm that stupid? Did you think I'd never find out?

DEVIL: You know, I can't live like this . . .

ANGEL: Still can't answer the question, can you?

You see how nicely that worked out? In just a matter of seconds, you can turn a potentially crippling Jedi mind game into a full-scale interrogation and walk away victorious. Now, are you ready to try this at home? Once you have successfully avoided or removed yourself from a Jedi mind game, you can get to the root of the confrontation. This is the point where you lay it all on the line (well, at least a portion of it). Once you have presented the elements of your case, you can observe and evaluate his reaction. In the next chapter, you'll learn how to interpret his responses so you can best determine your next course of action.

If, however, you find yourself deeply trapped within a Jedi mind game—if you have fallen and are having a hard time getting up—don't give up! It's time to resort to a different tactic and call his bluff. Make him verify his so-called story. This surefire tactic is a very effective one. Suggest that "we" call his aunt to determine if he really spent last night at her place, or that "we" check with his cousin to see if that new leather wallet really came from her. By directly challenging his story, you also have to be prepared for him to fight you every step of the way. He may counterattack by throwing a line at you like "I can't believe you are really going to call my aunt!" "Why would you bring other people into our private business?" or "I can't believe you don't trust me. I've had enough! It's over!" Yeah, yeah, yeah, make the call anyway. And make sure to do it right then, before he has a chance to call ahead and get his story straight. *Do not* under any circumstances allow him to talk you out of making that call! It's best to verify the story now rather than turn a blind eye to the obvious and continue to deal with it in the future.

KEEP YOUR SOURCES A SECRET

In Chapter 2, I touched upon the significance of keeping your sources of information under wraps. Because this is such an important point, it merits discussing in further detail here.

Revealing any source of information, be it an informant, a telephone bill, or a personal stakeout, is always a bad idea. Not only will this give your mate someone at whom he can direct his anger (if the source is an informant), it will also give him a heads-up, alerting him to cover his tracks better in the future.

There is always a way to explain how you obtained the information you gathered without giving up your source. For example, if you rifled through his phone bills and found that "her" number appeared numerous times, don't tell him how you came upon the information. Rather tell him that on numerous occasions (never give exact dates), you pressed the redial button on his phone and her number was displayed. Along the same lines, you never want him to know that you saw him entering his voicemail code into the phone, or that you obtained the code from the redial screen, because he will never allow that to happen again.

If you have obtained some incriminating evidence through an informant, particularly if it is someone your partner knows, it is crucial that the person's identity be kept secret. And don't let your unfaithful mate bully you into thinking he has the right to know. He does not. Obviously, he cannot deny the fact that he spent last Wednesday night having a romantic dinner with some woman he recently met at the gym. So when you bring it up, it really doesn't matter *who* spotted him that night. He *knows* he is guilty!

If, however, you feel more comfortable making up a story to protect the informant's identity, you can always claim that you were given the information by someone your partner doesn't know— perhaps one of your coworkers. You can say that he or she spotted your cheating mate and recognized him from the photo on your desk. (Of course, don't mention any names.) You can also choose to take the fall yourself, claiming that you followed him and actually saw them together.

No matter how you decide to handle this matter, never divulge your sources. Go to whatever lengths are necessary to conceal them.

And remember, I'm not just talking about people. Keep in mind that once he is aware that you have gleaned evidence from his telephone bills, bank statements, voicemail codes, and/or credit card bills, he will never afford you or anyone else access to them in the future.

TO SUM IT UP

After you have gathered all of the necessary evidence, remember to take a step back and remind yourself of the purpose of your investigation. Whether you will be using the facts you have gathered to say goodbye to your cheating partner or to give him another chance, this chapter has shown you some helpful strategies for confronting him with the evidence. In the next chapter, you'll learn how to interpret his responses so you can best determine your next course of action.

CHAPTER 4

What Now?

Now that you have played your hand and exposed the game of your unfaithful mate, what are you going to do next? Much of your answer will depend on the type of response elicited by your confrontation. The way in which your partner reacts to and deals with the evidence presented against him is crucial in determining the future course of your relationship. Properly evaluating your partner's reaction will provide you with valuable insight into the reality of the situation.

EVALUATING REACTIONS

No matter how solid your case, no matter how strong the evidence, there is always the chance that your cheating partner will not admit to a single thing. Even if you have a picture of him in a hotel room with another women, find a G-string in his car, and unearth a stack of love letters, he may still claim his innocence. If this is the case, do not be discouraged. You must always remember that your purpose for going on this expedition was to gather enough proof to uncover the truth *for yourself*, not for him! He already knows exactly what's going on, and chances are a lot of other people do too.

It is not important to convince your mate of his guilt. It's something he already knows—even though he may staunchly deny it. Don't waste your time! If you are satisfied that you have enough proof to verify your suspicions, you don't need his validation. Your purpose in telling him was to let him know that you are not a fool and you are on to his game. It was not to give him the opportunity to continue to play more mind games with you, forcing you again to question your sanity and what you already know in your heart to be true. When a person who is cornered with a significant amount of evidence still cannot admit the truth, it shows that he will do whatever it takes to cover his posterior. If he refuses to acknowledge or take responsibility for any part of his behavior, then there is little if any hope that the relationship can be salvaged. This also means that if your goal in gathering evidence was to shake him up and hopefully straighten him out, you may need to step back and re-evaluate the probability of that happening.

On the other hand, your mate may admit his infidelity and react emotionally during your confrontation. He may even break down and sob hysterically, telling you over and over again how sorry he is and begging for your forgiveness. He may also promise that this will never happen again while pleading for another chance. Of course, he may be sincere, but it is important for you to know the distinction between "I'm sorry for what I did" versus "I'm sorry I got caught." The first statement is usually more legitimate if it is delivered *before* you have confronted him with the evidence. Unfortunately, once you have presented your case, the second statement is likely to be more accurate. When someone is truly sorry for his actions, he is remorseful *at the time of the action*, not at the time of the confrontation. Think about it. Did he look sorry in the photos you found of them together? Did he sound sorry during the telephone conversations you overheard? Did he feel sorry as they slept together in the hotel room? Of course not, but how convenient for him to be sorry now that he's been caught! I'm not saying this to discourage you from the emotional bonding that may lead to a resolution, only to remind you to be aware of the reality behind the promises and the tears.

You may also find yourself dealing with someone who secretly wanted you to find out about the other woman all along. And now that you know, he finally has a way out of his commitment to you. He may have ended his part of your relationship a long time ago and just never bothered to inform you of this decision. If this is the case, you may begin struggling with feelings of anger toward yourself, questioning whether or not you should have undertaken this searching expedition in the first place. You may even become angry with your informants, somehow blaming them for the outcome. It's important for you to take a step back, pull yourself together, and take an honest look at what has occurred. There is no one to blame here except the spineless person who wasn't "man enough" to be straightforward with you. Instead of treating you with the dignity and respect you deserve, he chose to lie, sneak, pretend, and do his very best to make a fool out of you. You did not contribute to the early demise of your relationship, and you are much better off without him.

Finally, your mate may be the type to acknowledge the reality of what he has done, but somehow find a way to deflect any responsibility for his actions. He may try to give you some story about how he was stalked, assaulted, and raped by this crazed woman. He will expect you to believe that "She just showed up" and there was absolutely nothing he could possibly do but invite her to spend the night. Or perhaps he will not place the blame on the other woman but rather on you. He may claim that your constant nagging, long hours spent at work, or sexual hang-ups drove him into the arms of the other woman during a time when he was feeling vulnerable. What makes this type of statement so disturbing is that instead of working on the problem he was obviously having with your relationship, he opted to fly toward another window of opportunity. Let's be realistic. No relationship is perfect. They all have their challenges—some more difficult than others. But this doesn't mean that you shouldn't expect fidelity from your partner. If you intend to stay with this man, who chooses to veer from your relationship rather than deal with any challenges it presents, you had better seriously evaluate his stability and maturity. And if he tries to convince you all men cheat, cheating is characteristic of human nature, and he is no different from any other man, you should be very concerned.

Yes, individuals can certainly vary in their responses during confrontation. It is important, therefore, to view the reactions just discussed as more of a gauge for behavior than a guide for determining the future of your relationship. Only you know the intricacies of your partner and the issues relevant to your particular relationship. And only you can decide the direction in which you wish to proceed.

KNOW WHAT'S ON THE LINE

Once you have completed the confrontation process and evaluated your mate's response to the evidence presented against him, it's time to honestly assess the quality of your relationship and determine whether you feel it is worthy of salvaging. This evaluation process should not be done hastily; it should be given careful thought and consideration.

The decision you make at this juncture is crucial not only to the direction of your relationship, but also to the future of your own emotional and psychological well-being. It's time to consider all the things you will gain or lose by maintaining a relationship that has been marred by infidelity. Would it be better to work on preserving the relationship or to let it go? Several factors should be considered, such as children, finances, and religious beliefs. Do you honestly feel that your partner is capable of commitment? Do you believe you will be able to trust him again? Is it probable or even possible for you to be happy in the relationship again? While deciding whether or not to maintain the relationship, it may be beneficial to seek some outside help to give you a hand at sorting through your thoughts and feelings. Possible choices may include a therapist, a spiritual advisor, or an objective third party.

Although this decision should be made only after careful consideration of important factors relating to family and stability, many people base their decision on more shallow grounds. How many of the following reasons for choosing to remain with an unfaithful mate have you heard (or used yourself)?

"I am just *not* going to let that woman steal my husband away from me!"

"Aside from sleeping with other women, he's a good man."

"I have put too much time and energy into this relationship to start over with someone else."

"I'm not getting any younger!"

"For better or for worse, I take my vows seriously."

"I know that he really does love me."

"I want to have a baby before I get too old."

"I may not be able to find anyone else."

"He's my soul mate."

"He's just going through a phase."

"My kids really like him."

"But I love him!"

"Boys will be boys."

"I don't want to be alone."

Each of these so-called reasons for reconciliation has the potential for creating a lifetime of unhappiness and emotional misery. As shown below, each one is based on faulty logic.

"I am just *not* going to let that woman steal my husband away from me!"

No one can steal your husband without his permission.

"Aside from sleeping with other women, he's a good man."

Even Ted Bundy probably stopped his car at stop signs.

"I have put too much time and energy into this relationship to start over with someone else."

All the time and energy in the world does not matter if you're the only one who's putting forth the effort.

"I'm not getting any younger!"

But his girlfriends will.

"For better or for worse, I take my vows seriously."

But apparently he didn't, so why be the martyr?

"I know that he really does love me."

Love is not only a feeling, it's a behavior.

"I want to have a baby before I get too old."

What if the other woman feels that way, too?

"I may not be able to find anyone else."

But he certainly has.

"He's my soul mate."

Nothing a little therapy can't cure.

"He's just going through a phase."

Life is a series of phases. Is this how he copes with them?

"My kids really like him."

Hers probably do, too.

"But I love him!"

At the expense of loving yourself?

"Boys will be boys."

Perhaps it's time to focus more on the men and leave the boys alone.

"I don't want to be alone."

How many more nights do you want to lie awake and wonder where he is? Whether you want to accept it or not, you are already alone.

See the trouble with these reasons? When you are evaluating what's on the line, and determining whether or not to give Mr. Cheater a second chance, it is very important to consider the likelihood of finding yourself in this situation again. If your mate is already questionable, and you are taking him back for one of the reasons mentioned above, you had better open your eyes. The probability of finding yourself chasing him around and looking for clues in the future is extremely high. And while it is true that most people are willing to sacrifice or compromise in order to reap some sort of benefit, that benefit should be worth the sacrifice! So before you decide to have another go at your relationship, be sure that you fully recognize and prepare yourself for whatever compromises you will have to make to get this person back in your life. Make sure he is worth it.

THE DANGERS OF CAT AND MOUSE

After careful and considerable evaluation, you determine that the relationship deserves one last effort. Your mate may have gotten down on one knee, pled for mercy, and vowed to renounce his cheating ways. You found his remorse to be heartfelt and sincere. If this is the case, it is important to be aware (and beware) of a game called *Cat and Mouse* (also known as *Catch Me if You Can*.)

When playing this game, for which there are no rules and no real winners, each player tries to outsmart the other. The cheater continues to cheat while the sleuth continues to search for clues. The object is to continue to chase your mate around in circles for the remainder of your living days. During the course of the game, both the cheater and the sleuth become more sophisticated in their efforts to outwit their opponent. Eventually, the cheater will get caught, and the entire "confrontation-evaluation-I'll give you one last chance" cycle will start all over again from the beginning. And before you know it, the game is in full swing once more.

I truly understand the desire to regain trust in the person who has betrayed you, but you must first be certain that he is worthy of your trust. He must not be playing games. Think about it. Did you decide to give a second chance to someone who, during the confrontation, was not forthcoming with adequate responses to your inquiries? Did he refuse to give you information that you had a right to know? If so, you are likely to be a future participant in a game of Cat and Mouse. Additionally, if this is not your mate's second chance but rather his third, fourth, or fifth, then the likelihood that you have already played Cat and Mouse, and will continue to play the game over and over again, has increased tenfold.

Whether or not your mate decides to continue his cheating ways, there will still be occasions when you are likely to feel the need to randomly search for clues. Hopefully, he has reformed his behavior so there will be no more evidence. Consequently, your need to continue searching should decrease over time as the level of trust in your relationship increases. Hopefully, these random searches will become exercises in futility and eventually fall by the wayside. This is not to suggest that you should return to a catatonic state of ignorant bliss. However, once you decide to begin trusting again, you will have to give up some of those old sleuthing habits. If, however, you find that you are unable to take off the investigator hat, and continue to obsess over the need to find new evidence, then perhaps getting back into this relationship was not a good idea.

IN THE END . . .

So, as you have seen, the future of your relationship ultimately depends on you. You can decide to nix it as soon as you have solid proof of your mate's infidelity, or you can wait and base your decision on a variety of factors, starting with his reaction to the evidence. Remember, after careful consideration, *you* are the only one who can decide if he is worthy of another chance.

Chapter 5

Self-Reflection

I n the previous chapters of this book, I have provided you with some common signs of infidelity, along with tips and guidelines for gathering evidence to verify your suspicions. I have also shared some helpful strategies for confronting an unfaithful partner with the information you've gathered—for the purpose of either ending the relationship or giving him another chance to change his cheating ways. Most important, I have tried to stress the importance of "you" in this search-and-confront experience. Always remember that the purpose of your expedition is not to convince the cheater of his behavior, but rather to validate your suspicions to yourself.

If you have already gone through this experience, and your worst fears were realized, you may also feel somewhat vindicated, knowing that your suspicions weren't imagined—that you weren't being paranoid. In fact, you may even be able to rejoice in the fact that you are not being played for a fool any longer. The journey may have been long, tiresome, and sometimes maddening, but you had stamina, you were persistent, and in the end you finally won. But take another look. Did you really win? True, you may have uncovered the cheater for what he was, but at what cost?

I have known many people (myself included) who have gained the truth but "lost themselves" during the journey. You may have lost yourself, as well, and the signs are obvious: You haven't slept, you haven't eaten (or stopped eating), your nerves are shot, you've quit exercising, you've started smoking again, you're drinking excessively, you're biting your nails, your stomach is perpetually tied up in knots, you can't concentrate, you don't want to get out of bed in the morning, you start crying at the drop of a hat, you can't carry on a conversation about anything other than your situation, your health has gone downhill, and you haven't been able to give 100 percent to your kids, your job, or your other commitments. And you look like hell!

Sure, you may have won the battle with your partner, but at the expense of your mental, physical, and emotional well-being. Talk about infidelity. That's right. Take a good hard look—the reality is that *you* may be the one who hasn't been faithful . . . to yourself!

THE ULTIMATE BETRAYAL

I have often wondered why so many people (again, myself included) have subjected—and continue to subject—themselves to unhealthy relationships and commitments. Why is it that they allow themselves to spend countless hours searching, digging, probing, tricking, spying, hiding, seeking, and snooping? Wouldn't time be better served by believing, trusting, and honoring? Now you are probably wondering, "Believing, trusting, and honoring who? My partner? My friends? My marriage?" No, none of the above. I am speaking of you! Believing in *your* intelligence; trusting *your* intuition; and honoring *your* need for self-preservation. This doesn't mean if you intuitively feel your mate is cheating that it is absolutely, undoubtedly, 100-percent true. What it *does* mean is that you have a feeling there is a problem in your relationship. And you should take heed. This is the time to address the problem and attempt to work it out.

Why is it that we find it easy to trust our instincts in so many areas—our kids, our safety, our health—but not necessarily in our relationships? It is important for us to acknowledge how vital trust is for maintaining that bond. This means recognizing when there is a problem, such as infidelity, and then taking steps either to rectify the relationship or walk away from it altogether. Why do so many people choose instead to hide out in cars, search through wallets, and check dirty laundry for the scent of unfamiliar perfume? Although I wish I had the definitive answer to this question, I don't. What I do know is that it is more important to love yourself than it is to love the "security" of a relationship. The fear of compromising your standards should be greater than the fear of being alone.

During my own past experiences with unfaithful partners, I had often wished for the strength to admit, "This does not feel healthy. I think I'll step back and regroup now." But unfortunately, this was not always my reality. Like many people, I placed more trust in extrinsic, outside forces than in what I possessed within my own heart, mind, and soul. In doing so, I was unfaithful to myself, guilty of the "ultimate betrayal."

SETTING STANDARDS

So where do you go from here? Why, to the future, of course. It is time to stop dwelling on the past, focusing less on how you arrived at this point and more on how you are going to avoid going down that rocky road again. It's time to grasp this moment of awakening and seize the opportunity to establish some rules and standards for both yourself and your future relationships.

Setting standards means determining what you will tolerate as appropriate and acceptable behavior from your partner. It means knowing what you expect from him—which characteristics he must possess. At the inception of most relationships, we all have some notion of the qualities we would like our partner to have. But how many of those standards fall by the wayside over time? Once a relationship is underway, it's not uncommon for us to lower our expectations, compromise our standards, lose sight of that initial relationship criteria—to do whatever it takes to keep the relationship going. All too quickly we may find ourselves back in a disappointing place.

One way to break this maddening cycle is to maintain those all-important initial expectations you established at the onset of the relationship. They should be just as important to you weeks, months, and years later. Don't betray yourself by compromising what you feel in your heart to be important. Establishing and then sticking to those relationship guidelines will help you avoid problematic situations before they occur.

MINIMUM STANDARD OF CARE

The term "standard of care" refers to a legal principle that is used to gauge the expected behavior of people in certain circumstances. If a person's conduct falls below this established criteria, he or she may be held liable for damage or injury caused by that conduct. Although this standard was specifically developed as a legal principle, its concept can be adapted to everyday life as well as relationships.

I have established my own minimum standard of care list, which includes all of the qualities I feel are important in a partner. It is a type of mental checklist that helps me determine if a potential partner possesses the traits I feel are essential for a successful relationship. Before I share my list with you, it is important to understand that your list is likely to differ from mine—after all, we are different people with different standards and expectations.

Of course, it's always nice to find a handsome passionate lover with a great job, a terrific stock portfolio, a sexy physique, and a sporty car, but how long can the relationship last if he has none of the basics—the truly substantial qualities that are at the heart of a person's good character? Sure, I'll be the first to stand up and admit that I once chose a guy based primarily on his good looks and healthy bank account; but where did that get me? I'll tell you where, hiding in the bushes near his house at two in the morning, waiting to catch him with another girl. No, no, no. I am *not* going through that again! I will no longer sacrifice character for charm or sincerity for a handsome smile.

The following qualities appear on my minimum standard of care list. They have served me well in making positive relationship choices. Hopefully, they will also be helpful to you in establishing your own individual criteria.

☑ Honesty

Honesty is the number-one, most important characteristic to me in a relationship, *any* relationship, including those with friends, relatives, and coworkers. Over the years, I have had to deal with my share of dishonesty, and believe me, there is no bigger "trust-buster." I will immediately break off a relationship with anyone who does not possess the level of honesty that I deem absolutely necessary.

When making this all-important determination, I don't limit my evaluation to the relationship; I also consider how honest he is in other facets of his life. For example, does he lie extensively on his tax returns? While it's true that lots of people fudge a number here or there, does he take this form of dishonesty to a new level, claiming property, charitable donations, or children that don't exist?

How often does he call in sick for work when he's feeling just fine? Sure, most of us have taken an occasional sick day to catch a sale at the mall or spend a day at the beach, but does he always seem to be coming up with some ridiculous drama to get out of work? Generally speaking, does he own up to the occasional harmless mistakes he makes, such as forgetting a birthday or arriving late to pick you up, or does he tend to deny them? Does he cheat at games?

You may view some of these behaviors as harmless, but I believe they are signs of a dishonest person—someone I do not want to be involved with. But keep in mind that this is my list with my own personal criteria, factors that are important to me. Your list will be a reflection of your own personal needs.

☑ Respect

It is important for me to ascertain if the person with whom I am involved is respectful of me and my personal belongings, privacy, and space, as well as my beliefs and opinions. I know you may be thinking it's unfair of me to require someone to respect my belongings and my privacy when I have just shown you how to perform the complete wallet search; however, those search techniques are meant to be used only in a relationship that has already gone bad. Hopefully, by following the guidelines of your own minimum standard of care list, you will be less likely to hook up with a bad partner in the first place.

Not only am I aware of the respect a potential partner shows me, I also notice the respect he has for other people. And disrespect comes in several different shapes and forms. I find it particularly offensive to be around anyone who uses racial or ethnic slurs, or who refers to random people by derogatory names or titles, such as "bitches" or "fags." I once dated a man who constantly referred to women as bitches. It seemed as if every other sentence out of his mouth was, "That bitch at work told me . . . "

or "That bitch cut me off in traffic." He even referred to the actresses in movies and on television as bitches. It wasn't difficult to figure out that this guy didn't have a great deal of respect for women. So, can you guess the first thing to come out of his mouth when he became angry with me? You guessed it: "Bitch!" Now, you must be wondering if I continued to date him. I'm embarrassed to admit it, but I did—after all, he was tall and cute and had a great body. Did I regret it in the end? Absolutely. But as the saying goes, "I lived and learned."

Other signs I look for when assessing the respect factor is how he acts in public when we're together. Does he turn to look at every firm butt or well-endowed woman who walks by? Does he blatantly flirt with other women when we're out in public? Now, even the most straight-laced fella has an occasional wandering eye, but it doesn't mean that every babe who walks into the restaurant should get the full once-over.

It is also important for me to note if he acknowledges that we are *together* when we're in public. I have dated men who were taking their seat at dinner while I was still struggling to get out of the car in the parking lot. Additionally, I take notice if he raises his voice to me over a disagreement, or thinks nothing of causing a scene in public. To me, this type of behavior immediately signals that we are likely be dealing with respect issues in the future.

Each of these areas of respect is important to me. If you include this category in your minimum standard of care list, be sure to think about all of the behaviors you deem truly disrespectful and inconsistent with your relationship expectations.

☑ Communication

I have learned through trial and error that without communication in a relationship there is no stable foundation. The person with whom I am involved must be open and willing to talk as well as listen. I need someone who lets me in on his thoughts, feelings, and opinions; someone who keeps me in the loop over the everyday experiences of his life. I also need someone who is interested in listening to my thoughts, beliefs, and concerns; someone who is able to discuss all sorts of topics, including situations at work (mine and his), hot subjects on the news, and controversial issues.

I have known men who were more comfortable keeping their thoughts to themselves, their feelings and opinions under wraps. Typically, they also seemed just as disinterested when it came to listening. One guy actually became hostile whenever I tried prompting a conversation of any type.

Along with communication comes that all-important aspect of respect, which I have already deemed important. I expect a partner to respect my opinions even if they differ from his own. We should both feel comfortable enough to always say what's on our minds, including any concerns with the relationship.

For me, this basic level of human communication is essential. If I cannot talk with you, then I cannot be with you. It's really just that simple.

☑ Spirituality

I have strong Christian values. And it has been my personal experience that if my partner does not share these values, even to a lesser degree than I, it eventually leads to problems within the relationship. I have always tried to base my attitude and behavior on the belief that some day I will be held accountable by my Creator for each and every one of my actions here on earth. This spiritual belief always presented significant problems when I became involved with a person who felt accountable only to himself. Unfortunately, this generally translated into an "anything goes" attitude, resulting in behavior that was contrary to my spiritual side, my true character—and it made me uncomfortable, unsettled.

On the other hand, this same type of spiritual dilemma is virtually nonexistent when I am involved with someone who shares my faith in God.

For me, the issue of common faith and spirituality is critical for a successful relationship. It holds a secure spot on my minimum standard of care list.

☑ Friendship

If I cannot consider the person I am involved with a friend, then we have no business being in a relationship. In my eyes, a friend is someone I can depend on for direction and sound advice, not someone who will simply tell me what I want to hear. He is also someone I can feel comfortable enough to confide in without the fear of betrayal. I once shared a relationship with a guy who told his "other woman" *everything* about me. She knew about my medical problems, my family matters, and my workplace concerns. This guy not only betrayed me as a partner, he betrayed me as a friend. The bottom line is this: If I don't have enough confidence in a guy to share any deep, personal information with him, he's gone!

It is very important for me to feel secure in my partner's "friendship." It allows me to relax and be myself. If I can't let my guard down, I can't consider this person a friend, much less a partner.

☑ Loyalty

In my eyes, the issue of loyalty is intrinsically connected with friendship. I need to feel confident that this person is always on my side and in my corner. I must be certain that, if the need arises, I can depend on him to go to battle beside me, not abandon me. It is important for me to feel as if I am part of a two-person team, rather than finding myself on the playing field alone. If I feel as though he does not support me in areas I deem important, he's gone! If he goes out of his way to discourage me, tear me down, or compete with me, he's gone! If he is not on my team but always expects me to be on his, he's gone! And, most important, if he has greater loyalty to the time, friendship, or connection he has with another woman (yes, even his mother), *he's gone!*

☑ Commitment

One thing I have learned over time is that the degree to which a person honors his commitments to others is a pretty good indication of how he will honor the ones he makes to me. This is very important when evaluating the potential for longevity in a relationship. I always try to notice if the guy is the type who seems to get bored or tire of things quickly, whether it's his job, a project he's working on, or even a hobby or game. Does he consistently back out of the commitments he makes to the people around him, including his friends, family members, and coworkers? Is he the type who can't see a job or project through to its completion? Does he quit when the going gets tough or the task becomes difficult?

Ultimately, honestly answering these questions enables me to look at a potential partner and get a pretty good idea of his staying potential in a relationship. I once dated a man who was always involving himself in one project or another. At first, I took this as a sign of ambition, a positive quality; but I soon came to realize that he rarely completed anything he started, including our relationship. Forget about "for better or for worse, until death do us part"; I've learned that guys with commitment issues aren't likely to stick with the relationship after a few arguments. Forget about weathering any storms!

Yep, commitment is very important to me. I try to be sure of this quality in a potential partner before becoming too deeply involved. And if he shows negative signs once the relationship is on its way, I have no problem dismissing him from my life.

☑ Fidelity

Last, but certainly not least, on my list is fidelity. This one is really simple. If he has a history of cheating on women or the reputation of being a womanizer, it's obvious he has a real fidelity problem, and I steer clear of any involvement. If he was cheating on someone else when he met me, it pretty much guarantees that he will cheat on me with the next woman who turns his head. I don't care how gorgeous he is, or how sincerely he professes never to look at another woman again, I turn and walk away. Actually, I run for my life!

I have lived and, thankfully, I have learned. After finally taking an honest look at myself and realizing that I have had enough drama in my life, I finally started to see things more clearly. As far as assessing a man's fidelity, I have learned to read the writing on the wall. I am no longer foolish enough to believe I can change a person's inherent character. All the love in the world will not make a bad tree produce good fruit. Realizing that old habits die hard, I find it best to simply check this type of guy off the list and move on.

Well, there you have it, my minimum standard of care list. Although there are other characteristics and qualities I look for in a person, I am determined *not* to settle for a partner who is lacking in any of the areas on my list. Remember, these are my *minimum* requirements. After settling for far less than I deserved on far too many occasions, I am determined to avoid making the same mistake again. This is not to say that passing my little checklist guarantees a healthy, wonderful relationship; but it certainly allows me to get a better start out of the gate.

BE TRUE TO YOURSELF

Remember to always be true to yourself! It is so important not to "settle" in a relationship. By doing so, you will be compromising your standards, betraying yourself—the ultimate betrayal.

For this reason, I implore you to take the time to establish a minimum standard of care list of your own. Discern which qualities and characteristics you absolutely *must* have in a mate in order to be satisfied. Determine for yourself what you can and cannot tolerate and what you will and will not accept. Finally, it is imperative that you write down your list and *stick to it!* Doing so will set you on the best course for finding a lasting relationship—one that is built on a solid foundation. I wish you all the best.

Conclusion

While my obvious intention in writing this book is to provide you with practical tips for catching an unfaithful partner, ultimately, my greater goal is to encourage you to learn more about yourself. I want you to open your eyes and understand that by compromising your expectations in a relationship, *you* are the one who is the real cheater—and you are cheating yourself!

By choosing to be with a person you instinctively know is not suitable for you, or by allowing yourself to be toyed with in an unhealthy situation, you are ultimately betraying yourself. In addition, you are cheating your family, friends, and anyone else who depends on you to be stable and rational. No man, no moment, and no situation can determine your destiny unless you allow it to. And although you may find yourself stuck in a bad situation, once you find the pathway out—and you will!—you must be sure to learn from the experience. This means you must never forget to:

✔ **Go slowly.** Evaluate your needs and all that you desire in a relationship, and then take the time to watch, listen, and learn. Take an honest look at your mate's habits, patterns of behavior, strengths, weaknesses, character, morals, and values. Determine if any of these areas is in conflict with yours. If so, you will need to re-evaluate your reasons for continuing the relationship.

✔ **Love yourself first and foremost.** You cannot expect someone to love and respect you more than you love and respect yourself. If you act like a doormat, don't be surprised when people wipe their feet on you. You alone set the standards for what you will accept in a relationship; so if you don't respect yourself, no one else will either. Remember that no one can make a fool out of you unless you allow them to!

✔ **Never give up the essence of who you are.** This means not compromising your standards for any person or for any reason. If you are not happy with a situation, don't let a dozen roses or an expensive bracelet change your position. Never allow yourself to be bought. There is an old saying that goes, "If you don't stand for something, you'll fall for anything." Even if you're left with nothing else, you will have honor, dignity, and self-respect.

✔ **Trust yourself and believe in your instincts.** If it feels wrong, strange, or funny, it probably is. *Always, always, always* trust your instincts. Follow what you believe in your heart to be true—you owe it to yourself.

It's time to leave you with some final words. Never forget that strength comes from within—by following your heart. *You* are confident. *You* are strong. *You* have the power. *You* have the control! And always keep the following adage in mind: *Fool me once, shame on you; fool me twice, shame on me!*

Resources

There are a variety of websites that can assist you in collecting evidence, or can put you in touch with infidelity survivors who understand what you're going through. Please view the following websites as starting points. Because new sites are popping up all the time, you're sure to find further resources by using your favorite search engine to locate additional sites as they are created.

SUPPORT GROUPS

ChatCheaters.com

Website: www.chatcheaters.com

This site provides links to a range of infidelity forums, including Survivors of Cheats, which was designed for women who want to share the pain of infidelity.

DRB Alternatives, Inc.

Website: www.drbalternatives.com

Available to members only, this site, for a monthly fee, offers a community chat room for survivors of infidelity. A Message Board is available for postings.

Face Reality

Website: www.facereality.com

This site is geared for people at various stages of dealing with infidelity.

Marriage Builders

Website: www.marriagebuilders.com

Marriage Builders was specifically designed for people who are interested in putting their marriage back together again after dealing with issues of betrayal.

SurvivingInfidelity.com

Website: www.survivinginfidelity.com

This chat site—by far, the most supportive and useful one—allows people at various stages of dealing with infidelity to network with one another.

REVERSE TELEPHONE DIRECTORIES AND SEARCHES

Addresses.com

Website: www.addresses.com

This free directory assistance allows you to search by name, phone number, fax number, e-mail address, and more.

1st Source Investigations

Website: www.phonebust.com

Send 1st Source a small fee, give them a home or cell phone number, and they'll provide a wealth of information on the individual in question. This is a great resource!

Intelius

Website: www.intelius.com

For a yearly fee plus a fee for each search performed, Intelius will allow you to search by phone number, including cell phone number; or by name, address, or social security number.

Reverse Telephone Directory

Website: www.reversephonedirectory.com

Just type in a phone number, and this site will provide the corresponding name and address free of charge.

WhitePages.com

Website: www.whitepages.com

In addition to providing a name and address when you type in a phone number, this site will give you the person's name when you type in an address. All searches are performed free of charge.

SPY SOFTWARE

Blazing Tools Software

Website: www.blazingtools.com

The Blazing Tools website provides information about Perfect Keylogger, a hidden system that logs everything that is typed in a protected file. This system also carries out visual surveillance by periodically making screenshots.

Spectorsoft

Website: www.spectorsoft.com

Visit this site to learn about Spectorsoft eBlaster—software that captures incoming and outgoing e-mails, chat, and instant messages, and forwards them to the e-mail address of your choice. This system also creates hourly activity reports.

Waresight Spy Software

Website: www.waresight.com

Waresight offers Keylogger Spy, a key logger and monitoring program that allows you to secretly monitor and record a computer user's activities, including websites visited, windows opened, applications executed, Internet chats, and e-mail. This software also takes snapshots of the Windows desktop at set intervals.

Index

TWELVE MAGIC WANDS

The Art of Meeting Life's Challenges

G.G. Bolich

Magic exists. It is everywhere. It surrounds us and infuses us. It holds the power to transform us. It isn't always easy to see, but then again, it wouldn't be magic if it was. Counselor and educator, G.G. Bolich has written *Twelve Magic Wands*—a unique and insightful guide for recognizing the magic in our lives, and then using it to improve our physical, mental, and spiritual selves. It provides a step-by-step program that empowers the reader to meet and conquer life's consistent challenges.

The book begins by explaining what magic is and where it abides. It then offers twelve magic "wands" that can transform one's life for the better. Each wand provides practical tools and exercises to gain control over a specific area, such as friendship and love. Throughout the book, the author presents inspiring true stories of people who have used the magic in their lives to both help themselves and point the way to others.

The world can be a difficult place. Loneliness, disappointments, tragedies, and dead ends can sometimes seem insurmountable. Losing the magic in one's life can make it even more difficult. *Twelve Magic Wands* provides real ways to make it better—first inside, and then out.

ABOUT THE AUTHOR

Dr. G.G. Bolich received his Master's of Divinity from George Fox University in Newberg, Oregon. He earned his first PhD in educational leadership from Gonzaga University in Spokane, Washington, and a second in psychology from The Union Institute in Cincinnati, Ohio. Currently a professor at Webster University in South Carolina, Dr. Bolich has taught courses at the university level since 1975. He also provides private counseling, specializing in trauma resolution, and is the published author of six titles and numerous articles in the fields of psychology, religion, and spirituality. Among his published works are *Psyche's Child, Introduction to Religion,* and *The Christian Scholar.*

$15.95 • 248 pages • 6 x 9-inch quality paperback • ISBN 0-7570-0086-X

OUR SECRET RULES
Why We Do the Things We Do
Jordan Weiss, MD

We all live our lives according to a set of rules that regulate our behaviors. Some rules are quite clear. These are conscious beliefs we hold dear. Others, however, are unconscious. These are our secret rules, and when we do things that go against them, we experience stress, anxiety, apprehension, and emotional exhaustion— and we never know why. That is, until now. In this book, Dr. Jordan Weiss offers a unique system that helps uncover our most secret rules.

The book begins by explaining the important roles that conscious and unconscious rules play in our daily existence. Each chapter focuses on a key area of our lives—money, religion, gender identification, work, friendships, health, power, personal expression, marriage, and sex. Within each chapter, there are challenging questions for the reader. The answers provide a personal look at how we are likely to behave when faced with specific situations. Each chapter ends with an analysis of potential answers that is designed to reveal the extent of our secret rules.

Our Secret Rules concludes by explaining how we can use our newly gained insights to improve the way we feel about ourselves and others. For once we are aware of our rules, we can then learn to live within their boundaries, or we can attempt to change them. And as we do, we can enjoy the benefits of happier, more harmonious lives.

ABOUT THE AUTHOR

Dr. Jordan Weiss received his medical degree from the University of Illinois Medical School in Chicago. With an emphasis on the body-mind-spirit connection, he has worked at several leading complementary medical centers. A practicing psychiatrist for over twenty years, Dr. Weiss currently works at Irvine's Center for Psychoenergetic Therapy in California. He is the author of several published articles on emotional responses, and is a highly regarded speaker.

$12.95 • 240 pages • 6 x 9-inch quality paperback • ISBN 0-7570-0010-X

FALLING IN LOVE AGAIN

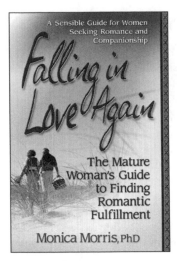

The Mature Woman's Guide to Finding Romantic Fulfillment

Monica Morris, PhD

Like millions of women, social psychologist Dr. Monica Morris found herself unexpectedly single late in life. The road wasn't an easy one, but Dr. Morris found her way to a new love. In *Falling in Love Again,* Dr. Morris shares not only her experiences but also the knowledge she gained along the way, providing an empowering resource for mature women who are looking for romance and companionship.

The author begins by exploring your expectations of finding love, thus preparing you for the real world. She then looks at the need for self-assurance and poise, and offers numerous ways to bolster self-esteem. Dr. Morris then provides dozens of sensible suggestions for finding that special someone—from personal ads to online dating to matchmaking services. Included are important details about costs, accessibility, and precautions. Dr. Morris even addresses intimate questions regarding sex, living together, personal needs, and independence. Finally, she provides a unique resource of services, websites, and organizations designed to help you find a significant other—or to just have fun.

There is life after loneliness. Both compassionate and practical, *Falling in Love Again* is your guide to finding a new love and a new life.

ABOUT THE AUTHOR

Monica Morris received an MA and PhD in sociology from the University of Southern California. Her areas of expertise include social psychology, sociology of emotion, and medical sociology. She was a professor of sociology in the California State University System for over twenty years. A widely published author, Dr. Morris resides with her husband in southern California.

$14.95 • 224 pages • 6 x 9-inch paperback • ISBN 0-7570-0136-X

GUY GETS GIRL, GIRL GETS GUY

Where to Find Romance and What to Say When You Find It

Larry Glanz and Robert H. Phillips

Nobody said that meeting someone is easy. But the fact is that people begin romantic relationships every single day. The trick is to know how to go about it, and this is the book that will let you in on all the secrets and get you started in the right direction. *Guy Gets Girl, Girl Gets Guy* provides all the important basics, including how to successfully meet, greet, and—ultimately—win that special someone.

Guy Gets Girl, Girl Gets Guy takes a practical look at the wheres and how-tos of locating and attracting that one right person. Part One focuses on who you are and who you want to be. It offers proven suggestions for enhancing your "inner" and "outer" assets. It then helps you consider and select the qualities you would like see in your future mate. Once you know who you are and who you would like to meet, the fun begins. Part Two provides a guide to the places you can go to meet new people—from the hottest websites to the trendiest night spots; from new and unusual places to common hangouts that are probably right under your nose.

This book even provides you with clever and effective ice breakers designed to launch your first conversation—a conversation that can lead to that first date, and maybe even a lifetime of love. With *Guy Gets Girl, Girl Gets Guy*, you have no more excuses to be lonely.

ABOUT THE AUTHORS

Larry Glanz is a relationships expert. He has spent over twenty years studying and analyzing mating customs in the United States. Based on this work, he has developed effective relationship strategies and techniques. He is the coauthor of *How to Start a Romantic Encounter*.

Robert H. Phillips is a practicing psychologist and the director of the Center for Coping located in Westbury, New York. He is the author of eight books and coauthor of the best-selling *Love Tactics*.

$13.95 • 176 pages • 6 x 9-inch quality paperback • ISBN 0-7570-0126-2

LOVE TACTICS

How to Win the One You Want

Thomas McKnight and Robert H. Phillips

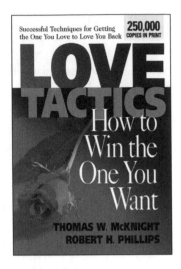

Maybe that very special someone is not as far out of reach as you think. Maybe what you need are a few effective strategies to finally make the right moves. Even if you're very shy, a little on the quiet side, or simply not the social success you'd like to be, *Love Tactics* may have the answers you've been looking for.

It's all here—how to build self-confidence, exhibit positive character traits, gain trust, and keep that special someone interested and hoping for a true commitment. *Love Tactics* will tell you all you need to know—from taking that first step and summoning up the courage to ask for a date, to sitting back and enjoying being with the one you want after you've won their heart!

Written in a warm, easy-going style, this book offers a wealth of practical advice on how to get the one you love to love you back. So don't just stand there—get out and stir up some hearts!

ABOUT THE AUTHORS

Thomas McKnight is a relationship expert. His columns on meeting the right person have appeared in leading U.S. singles newspapers and magazines over the past fifteen years. He has conducted dozens of relationship workshops throughout the country, and has also appeared on numerous radio and television shows, including *Oprah.*

Robert H. Phillips is a practicing psychologist and the director of the Chronic Conditions Center located in Westbury, New York. He is also the best-selling author of eight books dealing with various chronic health conditions, including *Coping With Lupus* and *Coping With Osteoarthritis.*

$12.95 • 208 pages • 6 x 9-inch quality paperback • ISBN 0-7570-0037-1